Mastering California Science Test (CAST) Grade 8

Based on CA State Standards, Next Generation Science Standards (NGSS), CAASPP Standards

Include:

- Review of all the science topics required for CAST Grade-8
- Practice worksheets
- Information about CAST test

Copyright © 2024 by Karry

All rights reserved.

Created and Published in the United States. This work, including all content, text, images, and illustrations, is protected by copyright law. All rights are reserved by the author. No part of this publication may be reproduced, distributed, or transmitted in any form or by any means, including photocopying, recording, or other electronic or mechanical methods, without the prior written permission of the copyright owner, except in the case of brief quotations embodied in critical reviews and certain other noncommercial uses permitted by copyright law. For permissions requests, please contact the copyright owner. Unauthorized copying or reproduction of any part of this work is illegal. Your respect for the rights of the author is appreciated. Thank you for supporting the creative work of the author.

About this book:

Welcome to the "Mastering California Science Test (CAST) Grade 8" designed to help the students, prepare for the California Science Test (CAST). This comprehensive resource has been meticulously crafted to prepare students for success in this assessment, aligning with the state's rigorous educational standards. With its engaging content, strategic organization, and ample practice opportunities, this book aims to empower learners with the knowledge and skills necessary to excel in science assessment.

This book covers all key content areas outlined in the California Next Generation Science Standards (CA NGSS), ensuring thorough preparation for the exam. Topics are presented in a clear, concise manner, making complex concepts accessible to students of all levels. It includes a quick review into all topics of Physical science, Earth science and Life science.

Ample practice questions and assessments are interspersed throughout the book, allowing students to reinforce their understanding and track their progress. These questions are designed as per the format and rigor of the actual CAST, providing valuable exam practice. It includes **multiple-choice questions, Constructed-Response questions and Performance tasks.**

"Mastering CAST: California Science Test Book" is more than just a study guide. It's a complete resource designed to support students on their journey to mastering science concepts and achieving success on the California Science Test. Whether used in the classroom or for independent study, this book empowers learners to unlock their full potential and excel in science assessment.

Keep Learning!

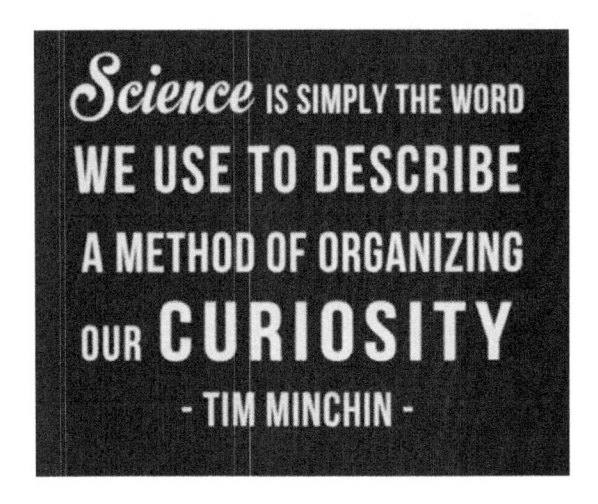

Science IS SIMPLY THE WORD WE USE TO DESCRIBE A METHOD OF ORGANIZING OUR **CURIOSITY**
- TIM MINCHIN -

Contents

1. Chapter 1: About California Science Test (CAST)................6

2. Chapter 2: Introduction to Grade 8 Science.......................13

3. Chapter 3: Physical Sciences..15

4. Chapter 4: Life Sciences..36

5. Chapter 5: Earth and Space Sciences..............................53

6. Practice Worksheets..69

7. Constructed-Response/Performance-Tasks......................114

8. Answers...136

9. Author's Message..148

Chapter 1: About California Science Test (CAST)

The California Science Test (CAST) is an assessment administered by the California Department of Education as part of the California Assessment of Student Performance and Progress (CAASPP) system. It is designed to measure students' proficiency in science based on the California Next Generation Science Standards (CA NGSS).

The CAST is taken by students in grades 5, 8, and 10, as well as students in grade 12, who have not yet completed their high school science requirements. It assesses their understanding of key scientific concepts, their ability to apply scientific principles to real-world scenarios, and their skills in scientific inquiry and problem-solving.

The test is computer-based and includes a variety of item types, such as multiple-choice questions, constructed-response items, and performance tasks. It aims to evaluate not only students' knowledge of scientific content but also their ability to analyze data, interpret information, and communicate scientific ideas effectively.

The results of the CAST provide valuable feedback to educators, and helps them in curriculum development, instructional strategies, and educational policies aimed at improving science education statewide.

Duration: This test lasts about 2 hours and covers life sciences, physical sciences, and earth and space sciences. The test can be administered over more than one class period or over a number of days.

Questions and pattern: For the first operational year of the CAST is a single test that consists of six Segments,

- Segments 1 and 2 will be made of 12 - 17 discreet items;
- students will be randomly assigned either another set of 12 - 17 discreet items or a performance task consisting of 4 - 7 items in Segment 3;
- Segments 4 and 5 will be randomly assigned performance tasks consisting of 4 - 7 items each;
- and Segment 6 is a student survey of 3 - 4 questions.

In short, students will have 44 - 60 questions depending on the number of questions in each segment (the minimum or the maximum number) and if a student receives the third set of discrete items or a performance task in Segment 3.

Cumulative test: *Please note these tests are cumulative that is 8th grade cast test will include all topics studied in middle school till grade 8*

In addition, student should be able to do data analysis, write explanations and use modals. Questions could be multiple choice or write responses or selection or drag and drop type.

Understanding the Structure and Format of the CAASPP:

The CAASPP in Science is aligned with the NGSS and assesses students' proficiency in applying scientific knowledge and skills to real-world scenarios. The test includes a variety of question types, such as multiple-choice, constructed-response, and performance tasks, designed to measure students' depth of understanding and ability to think critically about scientific concepts.

The test includes a variety of question types to assess students' depth of understanding and ability to apply scientific concepts. These may include:

1. Multiple-choice questions: Students select the correct answer from a set of options.
2. Constructed-response questions: Students provide written responses to open-ended prompts, explaining their reasoning and providing evidence to support their answers.
3. Performance tasks: Students engage in hands-on activities or simulations to demonstrate their scientific inquiry skills and problem-solving abilities.

Sample questions and format for CAST test:

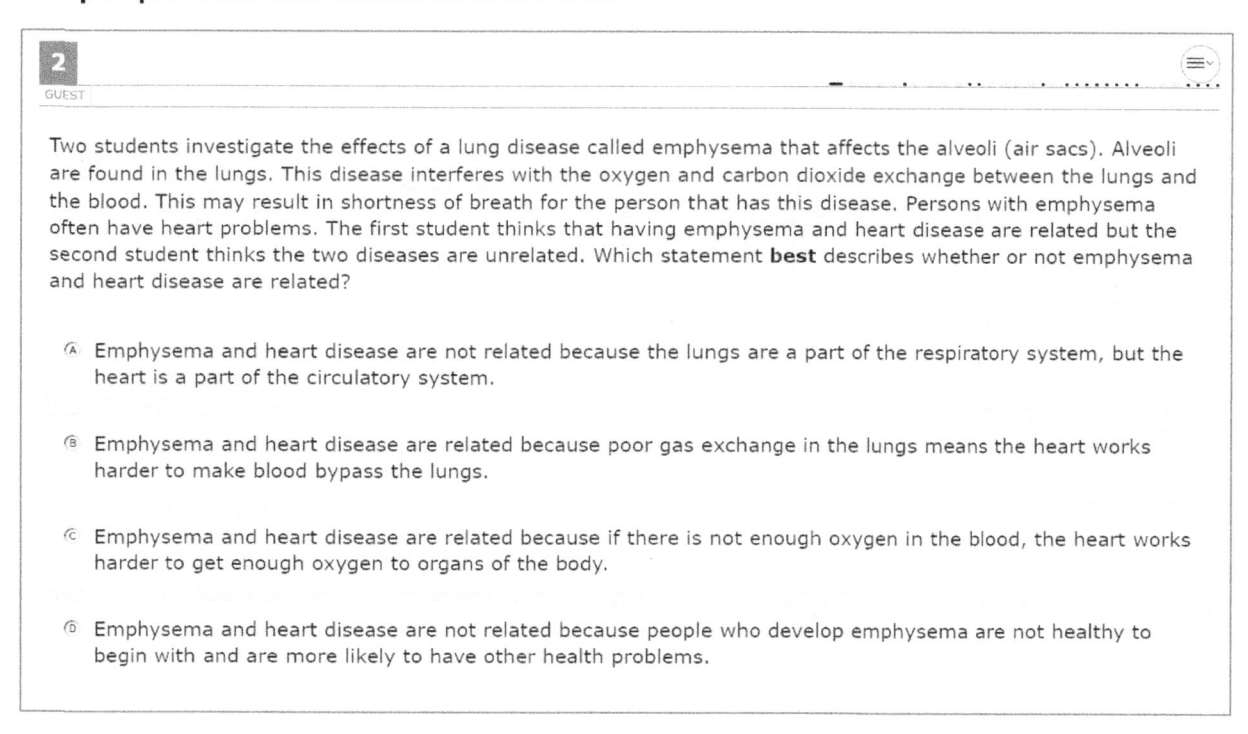

2
GUEST

Two students investigate the effects of a lung disease called emphysema that affects the alveoli (air sacs). Alveoli are found in the lungs. This disease interferes with the oxygen and carbon dioxide exchange between the lungs and the blood. This may result in shortness of breath for the person that has this disease. Persons with emphysema often have heart problems. The first student thinks that having emphysema and heart disease are related but the second student thinks the two diseases are unrelated. Which statement **best** describes whether or not emphysema and heart disease are related?

Ⓐ Emphysema and heart disease are not related because the lungs are a part of the respiratory system, but the heart is a part of the circulatory system.

Ⓑ Emphysema and heart disease are related because poor gas exchange in the lungs means the heart works harder to make blood bypass the lungs.

Ⓒ Emphysema and heart disease are related because if there is not enough oxygen in the blood, the heart works harder to get enough oxygen to organs of the body.

Ⓓ Emphysema and heart disease are not related because people who develop emphysema are not healthy to begin with and are more likely to have other health problems.

Glaciers are large sheets of ice found in areas where the air temperature remains cold most of the year. Students use a computer model to study how glaciers can affect land and living things. The students also study data that show that glaciers are melting rapidly.

Which changes to the computer model should the students make to show the **most likely** effect of melting glaciers?

Ⓐ Make the oceans more salty.

Ⓑ Cover some coastal lands with water.

Ⓒ Decrease the amount of water in the atmosphere.

Ⓓ Move animals living at the poles closer to the equator.

4

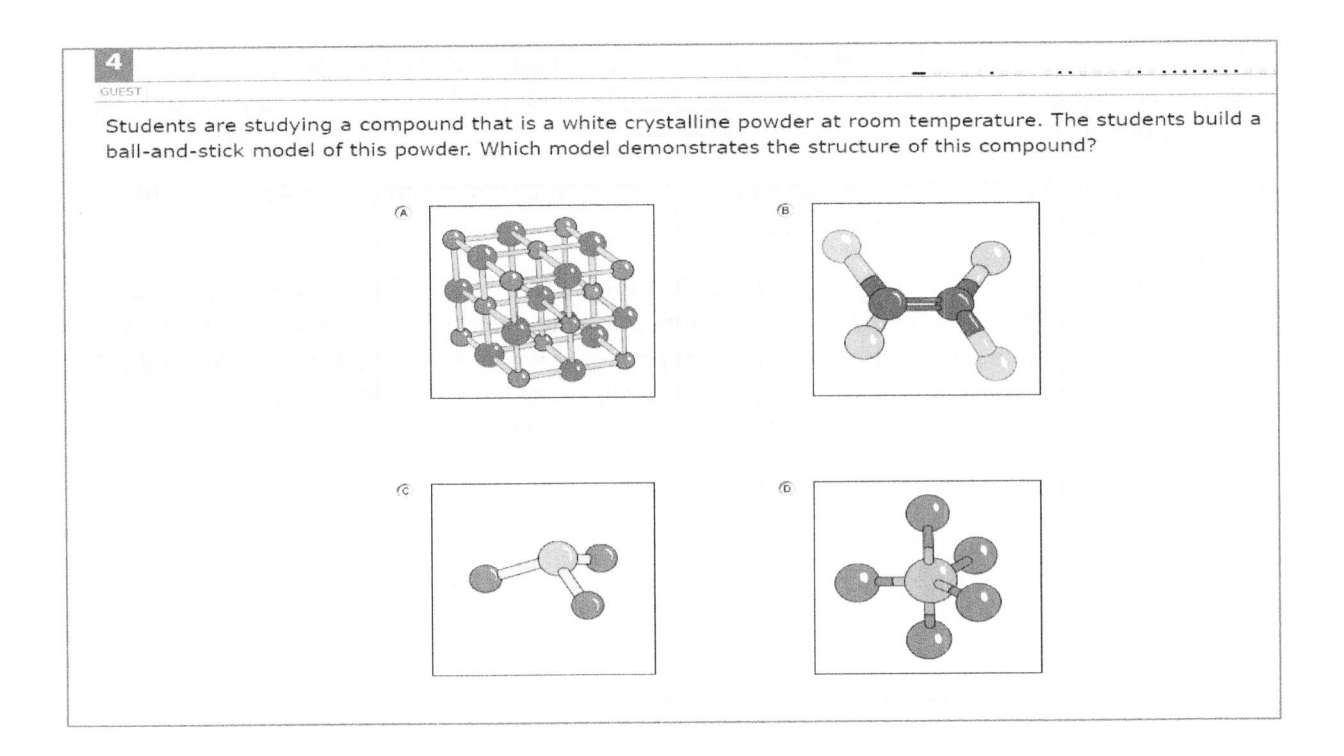

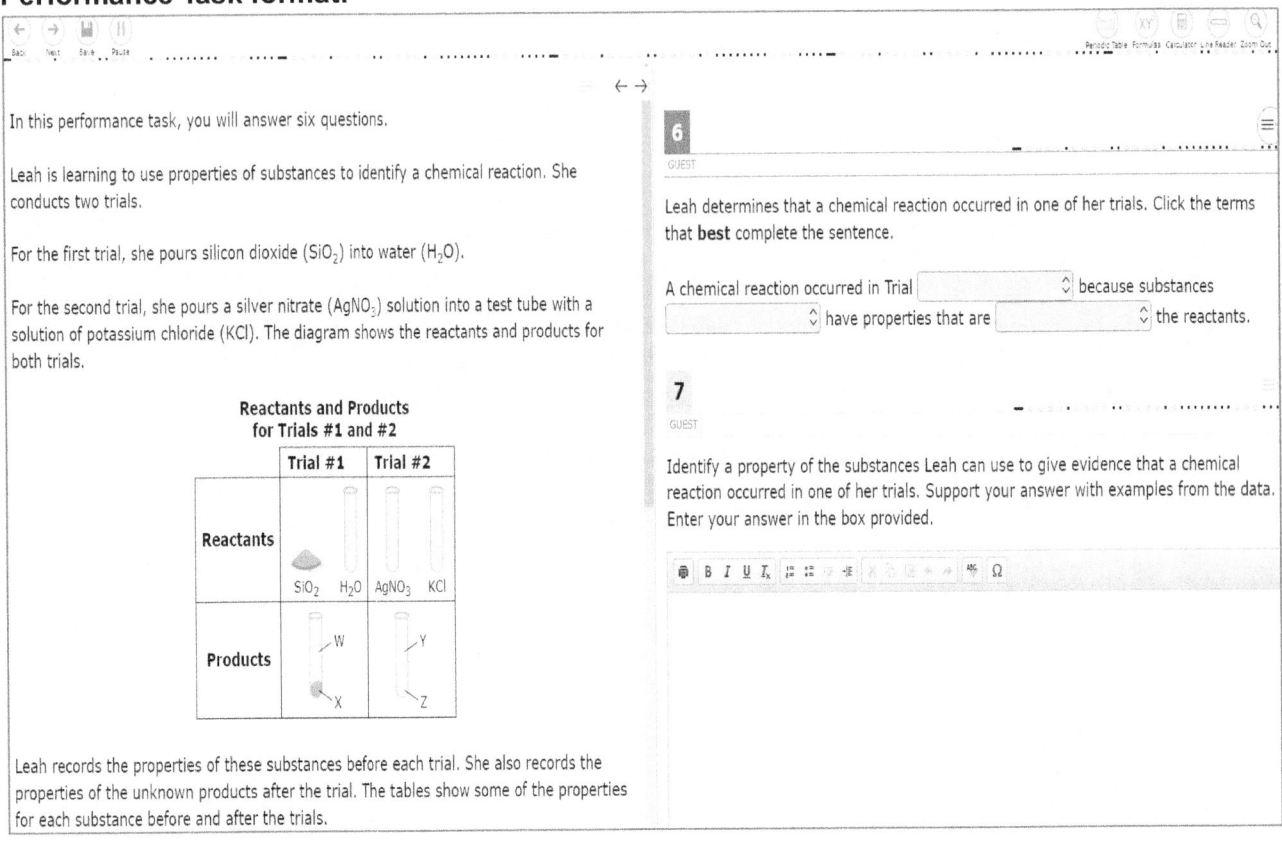

Students are studying a compound that is a white crystalline powder at room temperature. The students build a ball-and-stick model of this powder. Which model demonstrates the structure of this compound?

Ⓐ [lattice structure model]

Ⓑ [double-bonded molecule model]

Ⓒ [bent molecule model]

Ⓓ [trigonal bipyramidal molecule model]

Performance Task format:

In this performance task, you will answer six questions.

Leah is learning to use properties of substances to identify a chemical reaction. She conducts two trials.

For the first trial, she pours silicon dioxide (SiO_2) into water (H_2O).

For the second trial, she pours a silver nitrate ($AgNO_3$) solution into a test tube with a solution of potassium chloride (KCl). The diagram shows the reactants and products for both trials.

Reactants and Products for Trials #1 and #2

	Trial #1	Trial #2
Reactants	SiO_2, H_2O	$AgNO_3$, KCl
Products	W, X	Y, Z

Leah records the properties of these substances before each trial. She also records the properties of the unknown products after the trial. The tables show some of the properties for each substance before and after the trials.

6

Leah determines that a chemical reaction occurred in one of her trials. Click the terms that best complete the sentence.

A chemical reaction occurred in Trial [ ] because substances [ ] have properties that are [ ] the reactants.

7

Identify a property of the substances Leah can use to give evidence that a chemical reaction occurred in one of her trials. Support your answer with examples from the data. Enter your answer in the box provided.

Steps to practice Online Tests from CAASPP site

Step 1: Goto link https://www.caaspp.org/index.html

Step 2: Click Practice and training tests

Step 3: Click Student interface Practice and Training Tests

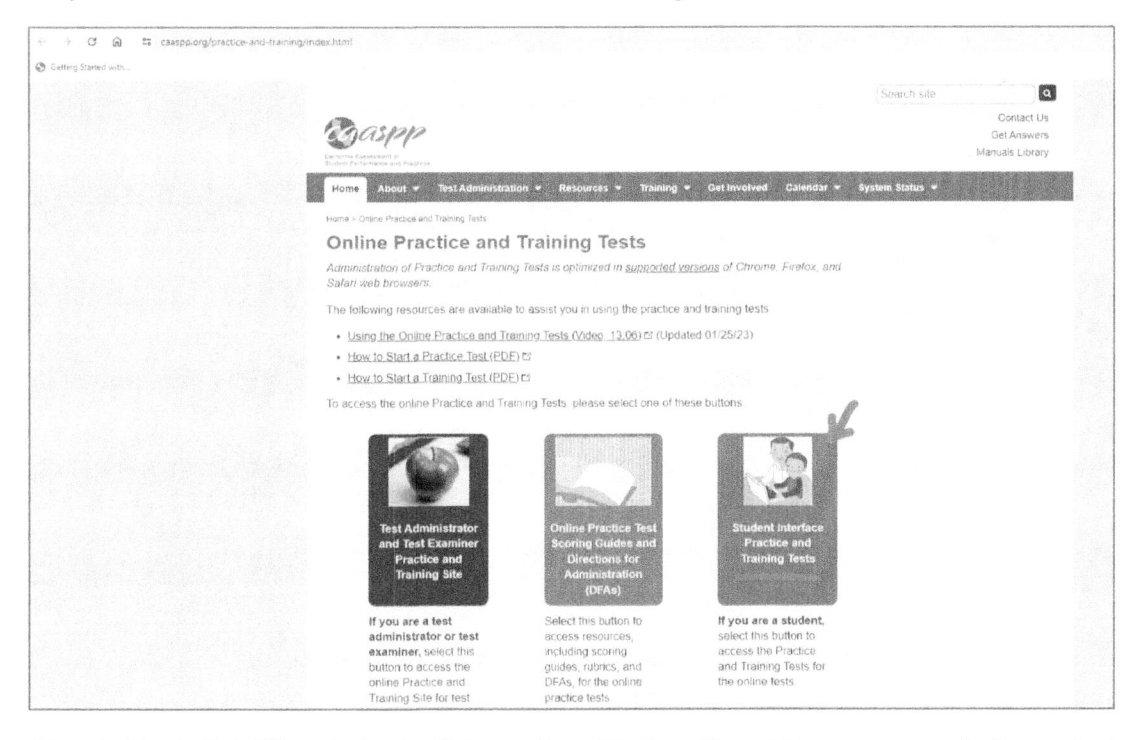

Step 4: Next click "Sign In button", keep it as "On" as Guest User, as seen in image below

Step 5: Then select the grade 8

Step 6: Then choose settings according to your needs. You can keep it default also. Then click "Select" Next check audio video, as seen in the image below. When you click on play button, you will see "I could play the sound and video" button turns green.

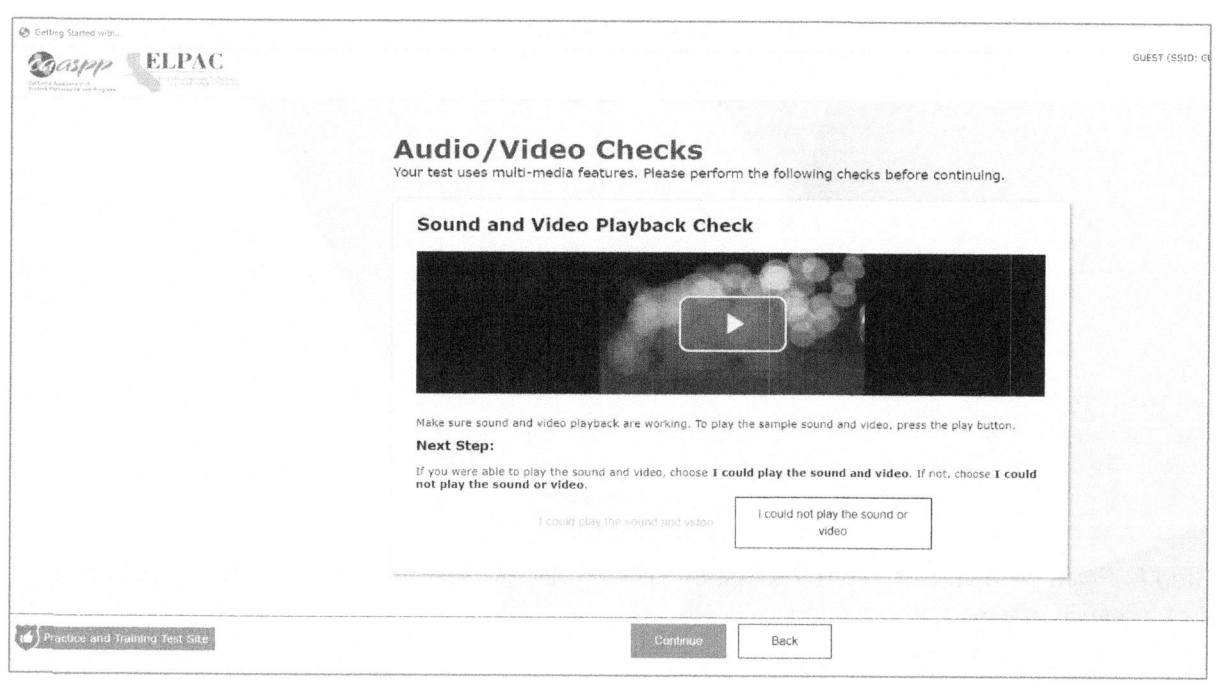

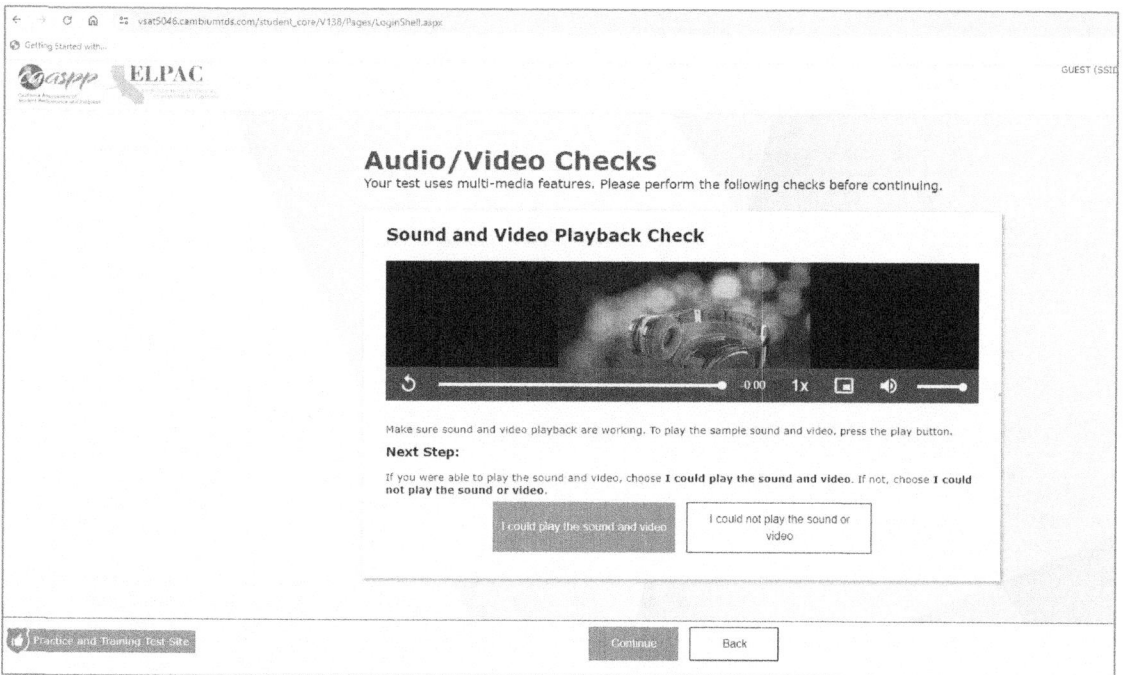

Step 7: Click "I could play the sound and video" button and then "Continue" button. Next you will see Instruction and help screen.

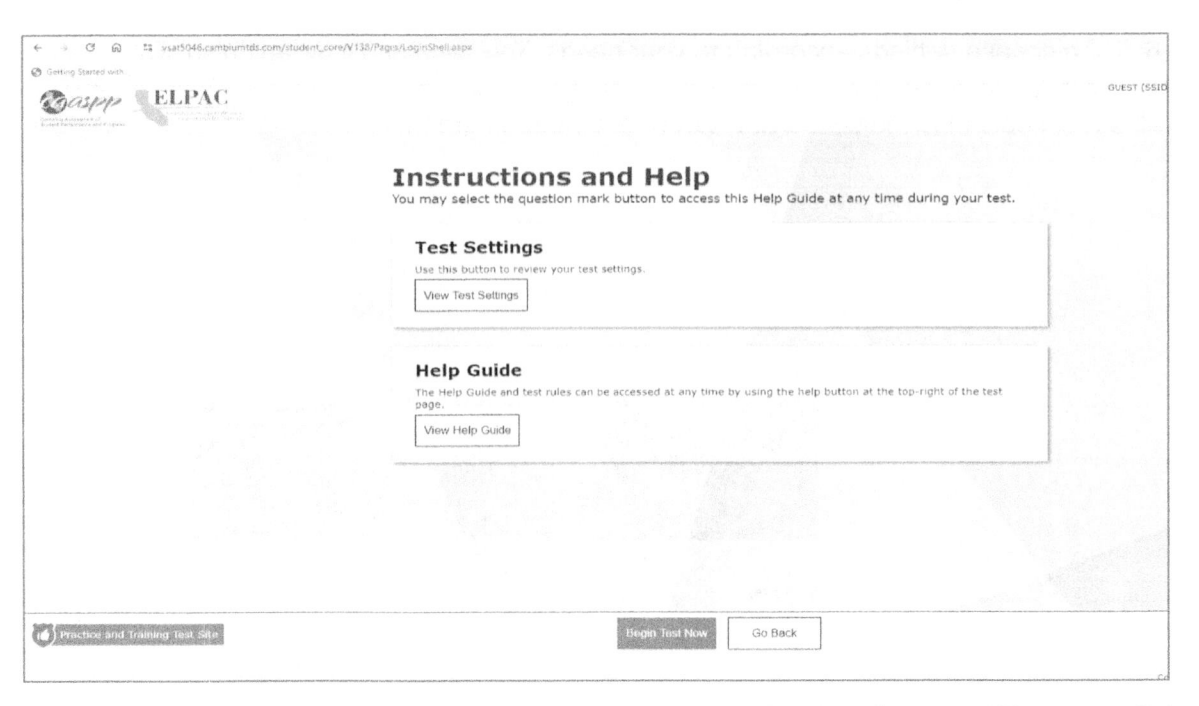

Step 8: From here you can start the test by clicking "Begin Test Now" button. When you click that, you will see the test question.

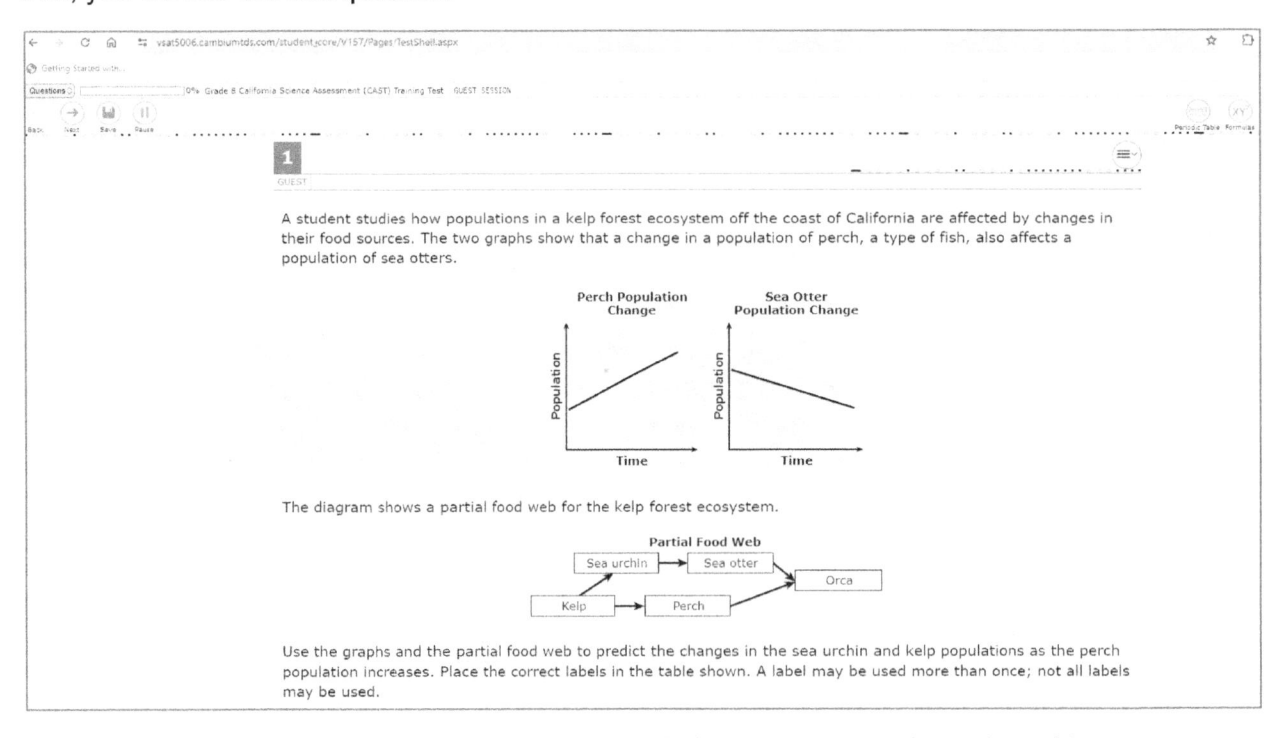

You will see multiple buttons to navigate on test and also percentage of test done. You can pause or save the test. Once you have completed all questions, you will see the message "Congratulations, you have reached the end of the test!" There will be "Submit" button, that student clicks and submits the test..

Chapter 2: Introduction to CAST Grade 8 Science

Middle school years are times for science exploration, where students delve deeper into the wonders of the natural world and develop their scientific inquiry skills. This introduction sets the stage for the journey ahead, providing an overview of the Grade 8 science standards and the importance of the CAASPP assessment. Since CAST Science test in grade 8 is cumulative, it includes all the topics covered in middle school.

In Middle school, students explore key concepts across the three main branches of science: **physical sciences, life sciences, and earth and space sciences**. These topics are covered in more details in the CAASPP Science test Grade 8. CAST test will include questions(multiple choice and constructed responses) and performance tasks from all these topics of science.

Introduction to the NGSS Crosscutting Concepts and Science and Engineering Practices:

The Next Generation Science Standards (NGSS) emphasize crosscutting concepts and science and engineering practices that are integrated throughout the Grade 8 science curriculum. Students learn to analyze data, construct explanations, and engage in scientific argumentation, fostering critical thinking and problem-solving skills.

The Next Generation Science Standards (NGSS) introduce students to two fundamental aspects of scientific inquiry: crosscutting concepts and science and engineering practices. These elements are integrated throughout the Grade 8 science curriculum, providing students with essential skills and frameworks for understanding the natural world and engaging in scientific inquiry.

Crosscutting Concepts:

- Crosscutting concepts are overarching themes that connect the different branches of science and provide a framework for understanding scientific phenomena. There are seven crosscutting concepts identified in the NGSS:
- Patterns: Identifying patterns in data and phenomena helps students make predictions and draw conclusions about natural phenomena.
- Cause and Effect: Understanding cause-and-effect relationships allows students to explain why certain events occur and predict the outcomes of scientific processes.
- Scale, Proportion, and Quantity: Examining the scale of objects and phenomena and understanding proportions and quantities are essential for making comparisons and analyzing relationships.
- Systems and System Models: Recognizing the interconnectedness of systems and using models to represent complex phenomena helps students understand how various components interact within systems.
- Energy and Matter: Investigating the flow of energy and matter through systems enables students to understand processes such as photosynthesis, energy transfer, and nutrient cycles.
- Structure and Function: Analyzing the structure of objects and organisms and how it relates to their function helps students understand how form influences function in the natural world.

- Stability and Change: Recognizing stability and change in systems over time allows students to predict how systems may respond to external influences and disturbances.

Science and Engineering Practices:

Science and engineering practices are the skills and processes that scientists and engineers use to investigate the natural world and design solutions to real-world problems. There are eight science and engineering practices outlined in the NGSS:

- Asking Questions and Defining Problems
- Developing and Using Models
- Planning and Carrying Out Investigations
- Analyzing and Interpreting Data
- Using Mathematics and Computational Thinking
- Constructing Explanations and Designing Solutions
- Engaging in Argument from Evidence
- Obtaining, Evaluating, and Communicating Information

By engaging with crosscutting concepts and science and engineering practices, students develop critical thinking skills, engage in authentic scientific inquiry, and deepen their understanding of the world around them. Throughout the Grade 8 science curriculum and the CAASPP assessment, students will apply these concepts and practices to explore scientific phenomena, solve problems, and communicate their findings effectively.

Grade 8 Science topics provides students with a solid foundation for success on the CAASPP assessment. By familiarizing themselves with the Grade 8 science standards, NGSS crosscutting concepts, and the structure of the CAASPP, students will be well-equipped to tackle the challenges of the test with confidence. Stay tuned for further chapters in this guide, where we will explore each content area in more detail and provide practice exercises to reinforce learning.

Happy studying!

Chapter 3: Physical Sciences

In this chapter of Physical science, we'll explore the fundamental concepts that you need to know to excel in the Grade 8 CAST exam.

Physical science is the branch of science that deals with the study of non-living systems, including matter, energy, and the interactions between them. It encompasses topics such as chemistry, physics, and Earth science, providing a foundation for understanding the natural world.

Key Concepts in Physical Science:

Matter and Its Properties:	Matter is anything that has mass and takes up space. It exists in different states, including solid, liquid, and gas, and can undergo physical and chemical changes. Students will learn about the properties of matter, such as mass, volume, density, and states of matter, and how to classify substances based on their propertiesalso about atoms, molecules and periodic table
Forces and Motion:	Forces are pushes or pulls that cause objects to move, stop, or change direction. Students will explore the effects of forces on motion, including concepts such as gravity, friction, and magnetism. They will learn about Newton's laws of motion and how these principles govern the behavior of objects in motion.
Energy	Energy is the ability to do work or cause change. It exists in various forms, including kinetic energy (energy of motion) and potential energy (stored energy). Students will study different forms of energy, such as mechanical, thermal, light, sound, and electrical energy, and how energy can be converted from one form to another through processes like heat transfer and energy transformations.
Waves and Electromagnetic Radiation	Waves are disturbances that transfer energy from one place to another. They can travel through various mediums (like water, air, or even a vacuum in the case of electromagnetic waves) and come in different types: Mechanical Waves Transverse Waves: Longitudinal Waves: Electromagnetic Waves: Electromagnetic Radiation refers to waves of the electromagnetic field, propagating through space, carrying electromagnetic radiant energy. It includes a wide range of wavelengths and frequencies, collectively known as the electromagnetic spectrum.
Chemical Reactions	A chemical reaction is a process in which substances, known as reactants, are transformed into different substances, known as products. During a chemical reaction, the atoms in the reactants are rearranged to form new molecules, but the total number of each type of atom remains the same.

Lets study about all these topics in details in next sections.

Matter and Its Properties

Matter is anything that occupies space and has mass. It's what makes up the physical universe around us, including everything from the air we breathe to the stars in the sky.

The study of matter and its properties is fundamental to many scientific disciplines, including chemistry and physics.

Here are some key **properties of matter:**

1. **Mass**: This is the amount of matter in an object, typically measured in kilograms or grams. Mass is a fundamental property of matter and is conserved in any physical or chemical change.

2. **Volume**: Volume is the amount of space that matter occupies. It's often measured in cubic meters or liters. Different substances can have the same mass but different volumes.

3. **Density**: Density is the mass per unit volume of a substance. It's calculated by dividing the mass of an object by its volume. Density is a useful property for identifying substances and determining their purity.

4. **State of Matter**: Matter can exist in three main states: solid, liquid, and gas. The state of matter depends on the arrangement and movement of its particles. Solids have particles that are closely packed and vibrate in fixed positions, liquids have particles that are close together but can move past one another, and gases have particles that are far apart and move freely.

5. **Physical Properties**: These are characteristics that can be observed or measured without changing the substance's chemical composition. Examples include color, odor, melting point, boiling point, and conductivity.

6. **Chemical Properties:** Chemical properties describe how a substance interacts with other substances to form new substances. Examples include reactivity, combustibility, and acidity.

7. **Phase Changes**: Matter can undergo phase changes when it transitions from one state to another. For example, solid water (ice) can melt into liquid water, which can then evaporate into gaseous water vapor. These changes involve the absorption or release of energy.

States of Matter:

Matter can exist in different states, namely solid, liquid, and gas, depending on the arrangement and movement of its particles.

- Solids have a fixed shape and volume.
- Liquids have a fixed volume but take the shape of their container.
- Gases have neither a fixed shape nor volume and expand to fill the space available.

Changes in Matter:

Matter can undergo physical and chemical changes.

- **Physical changes** alter the form or appearance of matter without changing its chemical composition (e.g., melting, freezing, boiling).
- **Chemical changes** result in the formation of new substances with different properties (e.g., rusting, burning).

Atoms Molecules

Atoms and molecules are the building blocks of matter, but they differ in complexity and structure.

Atoms:

- Atoms are the smallest units of matter that retain the properties of an element.
- They consist of a nucleus containing **protons** (positively charged) and **neutrons** (neutral), surrounded by a cloud of **electrons** (negatively charged).
- The number of protons in the nucleus determines the element's identity, known as the **atomic number.**
- Atoms are electrically neutral overall because the number of protons equals the number of electrons.

Molecules:

- Molecules are formed when two or more atoms chemically bond together.
- They can be composed of atoms of the same element or different elements.
- Molecules have specific chemical formulas that represent the types and numbers of atoms in the compound.
- Bonds between atoms in molecules can be **covalent**, where atoms share electrons, or **ionic**, where atoms transfer electrons to form charged species.
- Molecules exhibit distinct properties that can differ from the properties of the individual atoms they are composed of.

Particle motion and changes in state in Matter:

Particle motion is intimately linked with changes in the state of matter.

1. Solid to Liquid (Melting):

- In a solid, particles are tightly packed and vibrate in fixed positions due to strong intermolecular forces.
- As heat is added to the solid, the particles gain kinetic energy and vibrate with greater amplitude.
- Eventually, the thermal energy overcomes the intermolecular forces holding the particles in fixed positions, causing them to break free and move more freely.
- This transition from a solid to a liquid state is known as melting. During melting, the particles' motion transitions from vibrational motion within fixed positions to more random motion as they move past each other in a liquid state.

2. Liquid to Gas (Vaporization):

- In a liquid, particles are still close together but can move past one another, and the intermolecular forces are weaker than in a solid

- When heat is added to the liquid, the particles gain more kinetic energy, causing them to move faster.
- Eventually, the kinetic energy becomes sufficient to overcome the intermolecular forces entirely, allowing the particles to break free from the liquid and enter the gas phase.
- This transition from a liquid to a gas state is known as vaporization or evaporation. In the gas phase, the particles move freely and independently of one another, with high kinetic energy and significant distances between them.

3. Solid to Gas (Sublimation):

- Sublimation occurs when a solid transitions directly into a gas phase without passing through the liquid phase
- In solids with weak intermolecular forces, such as dry ice (solid carbon dioxide), particles may gain enough energy from the surroundings to break free from the solid structure and enter the gas phase directly.
- This process involves an increase in particle motion from the relatively fixed positions in the solid phase to the free and rapid motion characteristic of the gas phase.

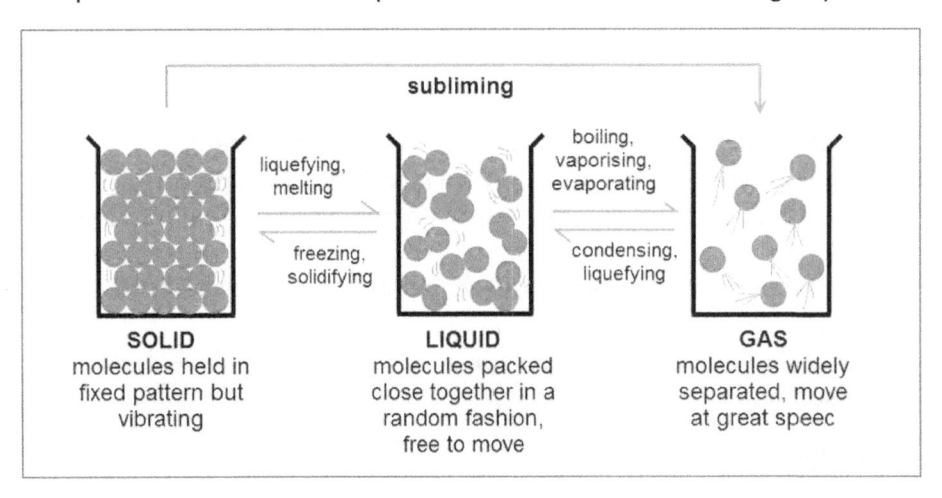

How does particle motion affect temperature?

Particle motion directly affects temperature through the concept of kinetic energy. In simple terms, temperature is a measure of the average kinetic energy of the particles in a substance. Here's how particle motion influences temperature:

1. **Kinetic Theory of Gases**: According to the kinetic theory of gases, particles in gases are in constant motion, moving randomly and colliding with each other and the walls of their container. The *kinetic energy of a gas particle is directly proportional to its temperature*.

2. **Speed of Particle Motion**: As the temperature of a substance increases, the average speed of its particles also increases. This is because temperature is a measure of the kinetic energy of the particles, and faster-moving particles have higher kinetic energy.

3. **Effect on Temperature**: When particles move faster, they collide with each other and the walls of their container more frequently and with greater force. This increased collision frequency and intensity result in higher temperatures.

4. **Relationship between Kinetic Energy and Temperature:**

- **Kinetic Energy**: Kinetic energy is the energy of motion possessed by an object. In the context of particles within a substance, it refers to the energy associated with the random motion of those particles. The kinetic energy K of an object can be calculated using the formula:

$$K = \frac{1}{2}mv^2$$

  Where: m is the mass of the object.   v is the velocity (speed) of the object.
- **Temperature**: Temperature is a measure of the average kinetic energy of the particles within a substance. It provides information about how hot or cold a substance is relative to a reference point. In simple terms, temperature reflects the intensity of thermal energy within a system.
- **Relationship:** The relationship between kinetic energy and temperature is fundamental. In a substance, as the particles move faster (i.e., increase their kinetic energy), the temperature of the substance increases. Conversely, when the particles slow down (i.e., decrease their kinetic energy), the temperature decreases.

5. **Temperature Scales**: Temperature is typically measured using scales such as Celsius (°C) or Fahrenheit (°F) in everyday life and Kelvin (K) in scientific contexts. In these scales, temperature is directly proportional to the average kinetic energy of the particles in a substance.

How does particle motion affect gas pressure?

Particle motion plays a crucial role in determining gas pressure. Here's how particle motion affects gas pressure:

1. **Collision with Container Walls:** Gas particles are in constant random motion. When they collide with the walls of the container they're in, they exert a force on the walls. This force per unit area is what we measure as pressure. The more frequently and vigorously the particles collide with the walls, the higher the pressure.

2. **Speed of Particles**: The speed at which gas particles move affects the pressure they exert. According to the kinetic theory of gases, the average kinetic energy of gas particles is directly proportional to the temperature of the gas. Higher temperatures mean faster-moving particles, resulting in more frequent and forceful collisions with the container walls, thus increasing the pressure.

3. **Number of Particles**: The more gas particles there are in a given volume, the more collisions there will be with the container walls, leading to increased pressure. This relationship is described by Avogadro's law, which states that, at constant temperature and pressure, the volume of a gas is directly proportional to the number of moles of gas present.

Motion and Forces

Motion and forces are fundamental concepts in physics that describe the movement and interactions of objects in the physical world.

- **Motion** refers to the change in position of an object over time relative to a

reference point. It can be described in terms of distance, displacement, speed, velocity, and acceleration.
- **Distance** is the total path traveled by an object, while displacement is the change in position from the initial to the final position, considering direction.
- **Speed** is the rate at which an object covers distance, while velocity includes both speed and direction.
- **Acceleration** is the rate of change of velocity over time, and it can be positive (speeding up), negative (slowing down), or zero (constant velocity).
- **Forces** are interactions that cause objects to accelerate or deform. They are described by their magnitude, direction, and point of application. Forces can be categorized into various types, including contact forces (e.g., friction, tension, normal force) and non-contact forces (e.g., gravity, electromagnetic forces).

: A force is a push or pull that acts on an object, causing it to accelerate, decelerate, or change direction. Forces can be exerted by contact (contact forces) or without physical contact (non-contact forces), such as gravity and magnetism.

Types of Forces:

Contact Force	Non-Contact Force
Muscular force	Gravitational force
Mechanical force	Electrostatic force
Frictional force	Magnetic force

1. The force that acts on the bodies in contact is called **contact force**.
2. The force exerted by our muscles is called **muscular force.**
3. The force exerted by a machine is called **mechanical force**.
4. The force acting along the two surfaces in contact which opposes the motion of one body over the other is known as **the force of friction or frictional force.**
5. Force that acts between objects that are not in contact is called **non-contact force.**
6. Every object in the universe attracts every other object with a force that is called its **gravitational force.**
    - Depends on the Mass and the distance.
    - Greater the mass greater the gravitational force.
    - Greater the distance less gravitational force.
7. Attraction or repulsion of particles or object because of their electric charge is called as **electrostatic force.**
    E.g.: -
    - Clinging of thermocol on palm, when cut with knife. [Attractive]
    - Rubbing of mustard seed in a polythene bag. [Repulsive]
8. Force of attraction or repulsion exerted by a magnate is known as **magnetic force.**

Basic of laws of motion, acceleration

The laws of motion, formulated by Sir Isaac Newton in the 17th century, are fundamental principles that govern the behavior of objects in the universe. These laws describe how forces influence the motion of objects and provide a framework for understanding various physical phenomena. Let's explore the basics of Newton's laws of motion and the concept of acceleration:

1. Newton's First Law (Law of Inertia):

- "An object at rest stays at rest, and an object in motion stays in motion with the same speed and in the same direction unless acted upon by an external force."
- This law essentially states that objects tend to maintain their state of motion (either at rest or moving with constant velocity) unless an external force acts upon them.
- **Inertia** is the tendency of an object to resist changes in its motion. Objects with more mass have greater inertia.
- For example, when you push a book across a table, it eventually comes to a stop due to frictional forces acting against its motion. Without these forces, the book would continue moving indefinitely.

2. Newton's Second Law:

- Newton's second law of motion states that F = ma, or net force is equal to mass times acceleration. A larger net force acting on an object causes a larger acceleration, and objects with larger mass require more force to accelerate.
- Mathematically, this law is expressed as F = ma, where F represents the net force acting on an object, m is its mass, and a is its acceleration.
- **Acceleration** is the rate of change of velocity over time. It can be positive (speeding up), negative (slowing down), or zero (constant velocity).
- For example, if you apply a force to a soccer ball, it accelerates in the direction of the force. The acceleration depends on the magnitude of the force applied and the mass of the ball.

3. Newton's Third Law:

- "For every action, there is an equal and opposite reaction."
- This law states that whenever one object exerts a force on a second object, the second object exerts an equal and opposite force on the first object.
- These action-reaction pairs of forces act on different objects and do not cancel each other out because they act in opposite directions.
- For example, when you push against a wall, the wall pushes back on you with an equal and opposite force, preventing you from passing through it.

The effect of mass on forces and acceleration

The effect of mass on forces and acceleration is central to understanding Newton's second law of motion, which states that the acceleration of an object is directly proportional to the net force acting on it and inversely proportional to its mass. Let's explore how mass influences both forces and acceleration:

1. Effect on Forces:

- Mass affects the force required to produce a certain acceleration according to Newton's second law (F = ma).
- When the mass of an object increases, more force is needed to accelerate it at the same rate.
- Conversely, when the mass decreases, less force is needed to achieve the same acceleration.
- This relationship is evident in everyday experiences. For example, it requires more force to push a heavy box across the floor than to push a lighter box with the same acceleration.

2. Effect on Acceleration:

- Mass also influences how objects respond to applied forces in terms of acceleration.
- According to Newton's second law, if the force acting on an object remains constant, increasing the mass will result in a decrease in acceleration.
- Conversely, decreasing the mass of an object will lead to an increase in acceleration for the same applied force.
- This relationship is apparent in situations such as driving a car. A car with a lighter mass accelerates more quickly than a car with a heavier mass when the same force is applied to both.

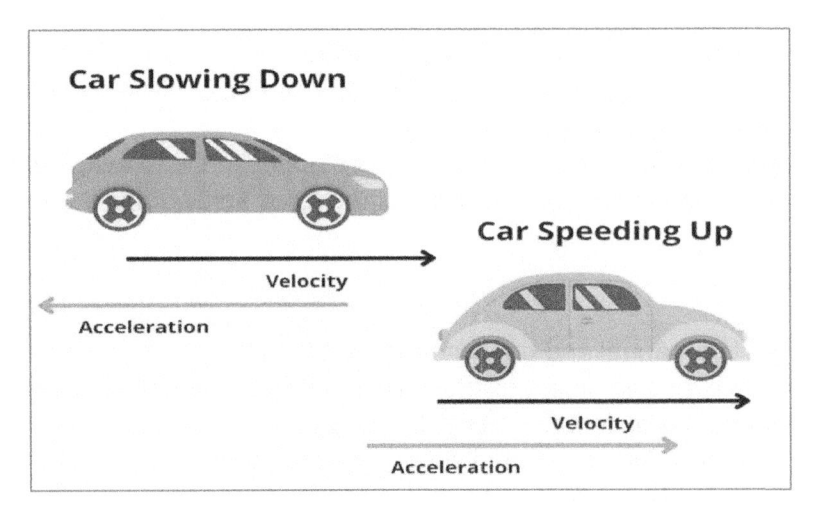

Balanced and unbalanced force

1. Balanced Forces: Balanced forces are forces that are equal in magnitude and opposite in direction. When balanced forces act on an object, the net force is zero. As a result of balanced forces, an object either remains at rest or continues to move at a constant velocity (which includes both zero velocity or constant speed in a straight line). Balanced forces do not cause changes in the object's motion because the forces cancel each other out. An example of balanced forces is a book resting on a table. The force of gravity pulling the book downward is balanced by the upward normal force exerted by the table, resulting in zero net force and no acceleration.

2. Unbalanced Forces: Unbalanced forces means that the force applied in one direction is greater than the force applied in the opposite direction. They can cause changes in the object's motion, such as acceleration or changes in direction. When unbalanced forces act on an object, they cause the object to accelerate in the direction of the net force. For example, when you kick a soccer ball, the force of your foot against the ball is greater than any opposing forces (like friction or air resistance), resulting in an unbalanced force that accelerates the ball in the direction of your kick.

Energy

Energy is often defined as the capacity to do work. • Energy can also be described as the ability to cause changes in matter. These changes can include motion, temperature changes, chemical reactions, and more.

Work, in physics, is the transfer of energy from one object to another, resulting in a change in the state or motion of the object.

Energy exists in many forms, including:

- **Kinetic Energy**: The energy associated with the motion of an object. It depends on both the mass and velocity of the object.
- **Potential Energy**: The energy stored in an object due to its position or state. Examples include gravitational potential energy, elastic potential energy, and chemical potential energy.
- **Thermal Energy**: The internal energy of a system due to the random motion of its particles. It is associated with temperature and is a form of kinetic energy at the microscopic level.
- **Chemical Energy**: Energy stored within chemical bonds of molecules. It can be released or absorbed during chemical reactions.
- **Electrical Energy**: Energy associated with the movement of electrons in an electrical circuit
- **Nuclear Energy**: Energy stored in the nucleus of an atom and released during nuclear reactions.
- **Light Energy**: Energy carried by electromagnetic waves, including visible light, infrared radiation, ultraviolet radiation, etc.
- **Sound Energy**: Energy associated with the vibration of particles in a medium, producing

Kinetic, potential and thermal energy

Kinetic Energy: • Kinetic energy is the energy associated with the motion of an object. It depends on both the mass m of the object and its velocity v. Mathematically, kinetic energy (KE) is calculated using the formula:

$$K = \frac{1}{2}mv^2$$

Kinetic energy increases with both mass and velocity. Doubling the mass doubles the kinetic energy, while doubling the velocity quadruples the kinetic energy.

*The unit of kinetic energy is **joules (J) in the International System of Units (SI).***

Potential Energy: Potential energy is the energy stored in an object due to its position or state. It is associated with the potential to do work. • There are different types of potential energy:

- **Gravitational Potential Energy**: Associated with the position of an object relative to a reference point in a gravitational field. Its formula is:
  GPE=mgh
  where m is the mass of the object, g is the acceleration due to gravity, and hh is the height above the reference point.
- **Elastic Potential Energy**: Associated with the deformation of an elastic object, such as a spring or a rubber band. Its formula is:
  EPE=½kx²   where k is the spring constant and x is the displacement from the equilibrium position.

Potential energy can be converted into kinetic energy and vice versa, depending on the circumstances. For example, when you drop an object, its gravitational potential energy decreases while its kinetic energy increases.

Increase in kinetic energy results in decrease in potential energy. Increase in potential energy results in decrease in kinetic energy.

Thermal Energy: Thermal energy is the internal energy of a system due to the random motion of its particles (atoms and molecules). In everyday language, thermal energy is often referred to as heat.

• It is related to the temperature of the system and is a form of kinetic energy at the microscopic level. The total thermal energy of a system depends on factors such as the number of particles, their mass, and their average kinetic energy (which is related to temperature).

• Thermal energy is transferred between systems through processes such as conduction, convection, and radiation.

- Conduction requires contact.
- Convection requires fluid flow.
- Radiation does not require any medium.

Conduction is heat transfer directly between neighboring atoms or molecules. Usually, it is heat transfer through a solid. For example, the metal handle of a pan on a stove becomes hot due to convection. Touching the hot pan conducts heat to your hand.

Convection is heat transfer via the movement of a fluid, such as air or water. Heating water on a stove is a good example. The water at the top of the pot becomes hot because water near the heat source rises. Another example is the movement of air around a campfire. Hot air rises, transferring heat upward. Meanwhile, the partial vacuum left by this movement draws in cool outside air that feeds the fire with fresh oxygen.

Radiation is the emission of electromagnetic radiation. While it occurs through a medium, it does not require one. For example, it's warm outside on a sunny day because solar radiation crosses space and heats the atmosphere. The burner element of a stove also emits radiation. However, some heat from a burner comes from conduction between the hot element and a metal pan. Most real-life processes involve multiple forms of heat transfer.

Heat Transfer

Conduction - transfer of energy between adjacent molecules

Convection - movement of a hot fluid

Radiation - emission of electromagnetic rays

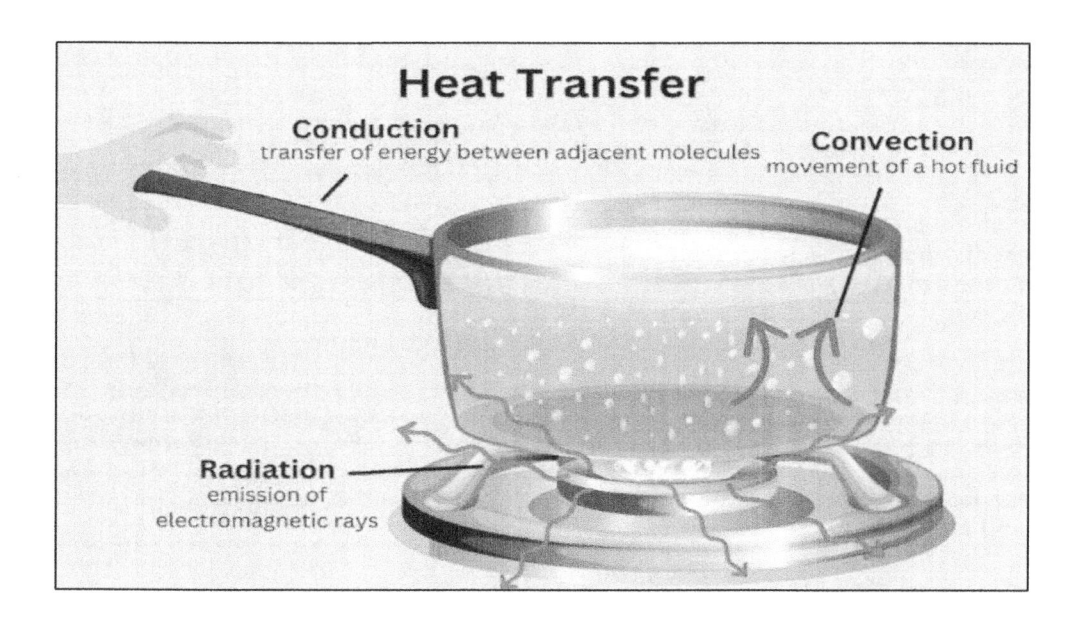

Energy transformations

Mechanical to Thermal:	When you rub your hands together, mechanical energy is transformed into thermal energy due to friction between your hands. The kinetic energy of your moving hands is converted into heat energy, warming your hands.
Chemical to Thermal:	When you burn wood in a fireplace, chemical energy stored in the wood is converted into thermal energy and light energy. The heat produced warms the surroundings, while the light energy emitted contributes to illumination.
Electrical to Thermal:	When you use an electric heater, electrical energy from the power source is converted into thermal energy. The electric current passing through the heater's resistor generates heat, raising the temperature of the surrounding air.
Kinetic to Potential and Vice Versa:	When you throw a ball upward, kinetic energy from your arm's motion is gradually converted into gravitational potential energy as the ball rises against the force of gravity. At the peak of its trajectory, the ball has maximum potential energy and zero kinetic energy. As the ball falls back down, potential energy is converted back into kinetic energy
Nuclear to Thermal and Electrical: •	In a nuclear power plant, nuclear energy released from nuclear reactions (such as fission or fusion) is converted into thermal energy. This thermal energy is then used to generate steam, which drives turbines to produce electrical energy.
Light to Electrical	In a solar photovoltaic (PV) system, sunlight is converted into electrical. Solar panels contain photovoltaic cells that absorb sunlight and convert its energy into electrical energy through the photovoltaic effect.
Kinetic to Sound	When you strike a bell, kinetic energy from your hand's motion is transformed into sound energy. The vibration of the bell produces sound waves that propagate through the air.
Potential to Kinetic (Gravitational):	In a roller coaster ride, potential energy is converted into kinetic energy as the coaster car descends from a height. As the car climbs a hill, kinetic energy is transformed back into potential energy.

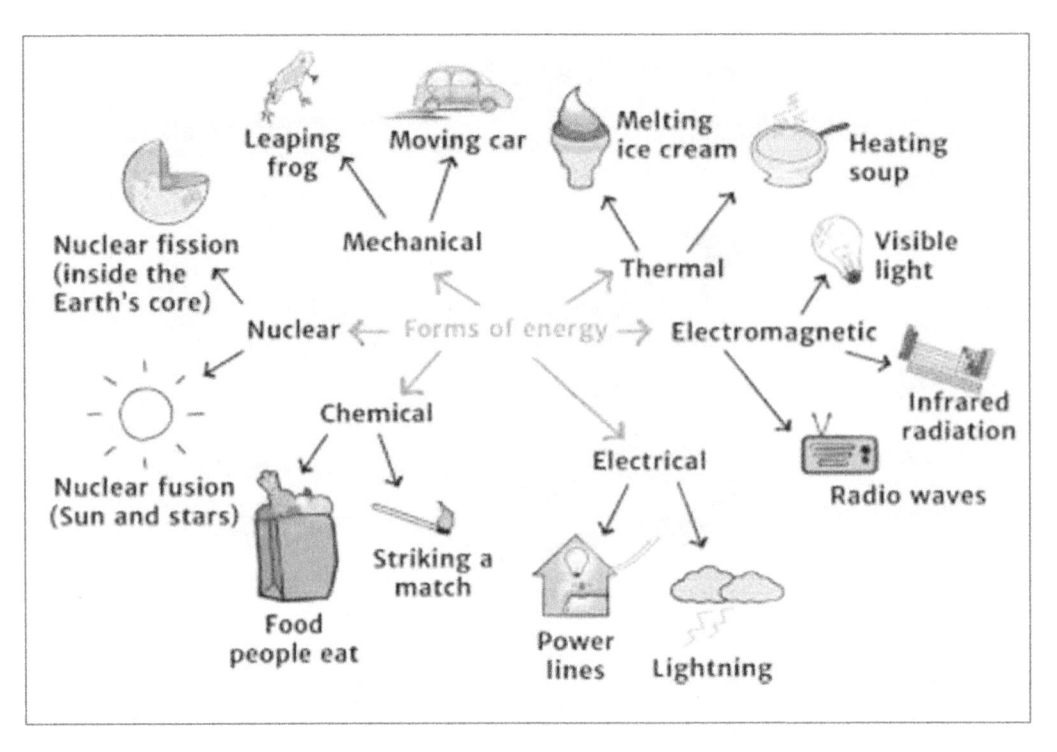

Conservation of Energy: • The law of conservation of energy states that energy cannot be created or destroyed; it can only be transformed from one form to another or transferred from one object to another.

• This principle is fundamental in understanding the behavior of systems and processes in nature. It allows scientists to analyze energy transformations and predict the outcomes of various phenomena.

Waves and Electromagnetic Radiation

Waves are disturbances that transfer energy from one place to another. They can travel through various mediums (like water, air, or even a vacuum in the case of electromagnetic waves) and come in different types: Mechanical Waves Transverse Waves: Longitudinal Waves: Electromagnetic Waves:

Electromagnetic Radiation refers to waves of the electromagnetic field, propagating through space, carrying electromagnetic radiant energy. It includes a wide range of wavelengths and frequencies, collectively known as the electromagnetic spectrum.

Wavelength, frequencies

Wavelength: Wavelength (λ) is the distance between two consecutive points on a wave that are in phase, meaning they are at the same point in their cycle of motion. In other words, it is the distance between two successive peaks (or troughs) of a wave.

Frequency: Frequency (f) is the number of wave cycles that pass a given point in one second. It is measured in hertz (Hz), where 1 Hz equals one cycle per second.

Relationship between Wavelength and Frequency:

- There is an inverse relationship between wavelength and frequency: as wavelength increases, frequency decreases, and vice versa.
- This relationship is described by the wave equation: $c=\lambda f$, where c is the speed of the wave, λ is the wavelength, and f is the frequency.
- For example, in sound waves, longer wavelengths correspond to lower pitches (lower frequencies), while shorter wavelengths correspond to higher pitches (higher frequencies). In electromagnetic waves, such as light, longer wavelengths correspond to lower energy (e.g., red light), while shorter wavelengths correspond to higher energy (e.g., blue light).

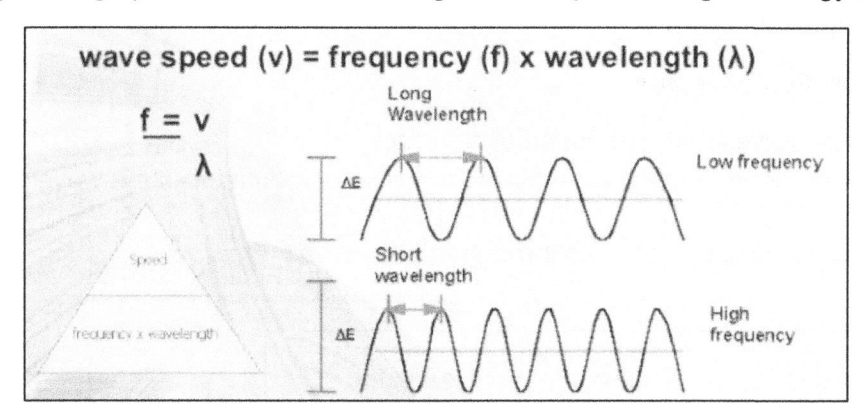

Energy of waves Transmission

In the context of waves, particularly electromagnetic waves such as light, sound, or radio waves, energy transmission refers to the process of energy being carried from one place to another through the propagation of waves. Let's explore this concept:

Electromagnetic Waves:

• Electromagnetic waves are a form of energy transmission that do not require a medium to propagate. They can travel through vacuum (like outer space) as well as through materials such as air, water, and solids.

• Electromagnetic waves consist of electric and magnetic fields oscillating perpendicular to each other and to the direction of wave propagation.

• Examples of electromagnetic waves include visible light, radio waves, microwaves, infrared radiation, ultraviolet radiation, X-rays, and gamma rays.

Energy Carried by Waves:

• Waves carry energy as they propagate through space or a medium. This energy can be transferred from one location to another without the physical movement of matter.

• The energy carried by a wave is proportional to its amplitude squared. Higher-amplitude waves carry more energy than lower-amplitude waves.

• For example, in electromagnetic waves, the intensity of light (brightness) depends on the energy carried by the wave. Brighter light corresponds to higher energy.

Transmission of Energy:

• When waves encounter a boundary between two different materials or mediums, they can be transmitted, reflected, or absorbed.

In the case of transmission, the wave passes through the boundary and continues propagating in the new medium. The amount of energy transmitted depends on factors such as the properties of the materials involved and the angle of incidence.

• For example, when light waves pass from air into water, some of the energy is transmitted into the water, allowing us to see objects underwater. The amount of energy transmitted depends on the refractive indices of air and water.

Reflection, and absorption of waves

- Reflected waves- waves that bounce off of a surface.
- Absorbed waves- the transfer of the energy from a wave to matter as the wave passes through it.
- Transmitted waves- waves that pass through matter.

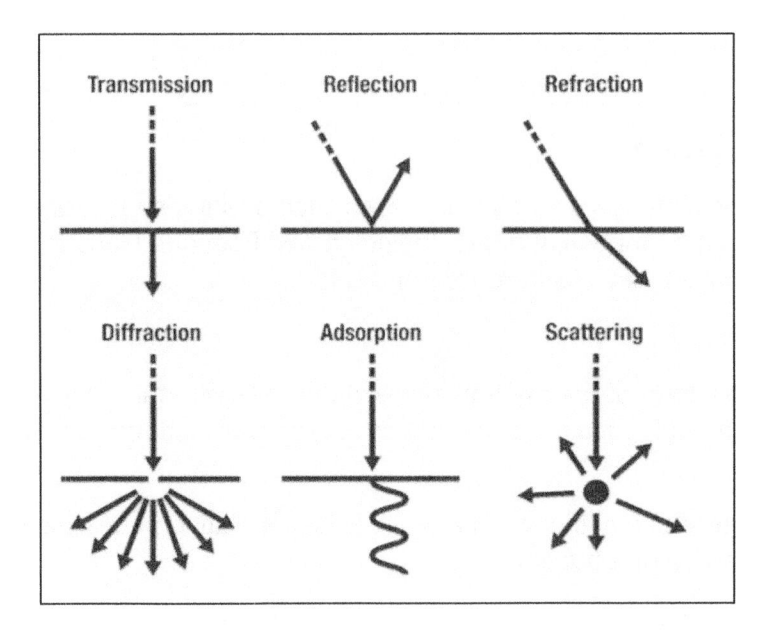

How do we see the color?

The human eye and brain together translate light into color. Newton observed that color is not inherent in objects. Rather, the surface of an object reflects some colors and absorbs all the others. We perceive only the reflected colors.

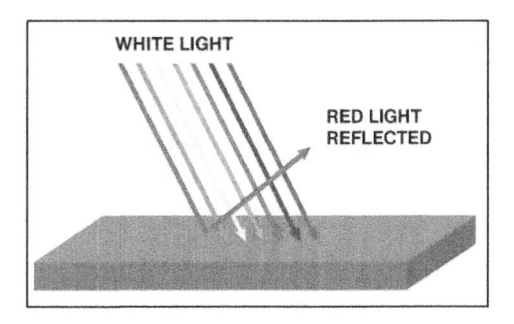

Thus, red is not "in" an apple. The surface of the apple is reflecting the wavelengths we see as red and absorbing all the rest. An object appears white when it reflects all wavelengths and black when it absorbs them all.

Transverse waves

Transverse wave, motion in which all points on a wave oscillate along paths at right angles to the direction of the wave's advance. Surface ripples on water, seismic *S* (secondary) waves, and electromagnetic (*e.g.,* radio and light) waves are examples of transverse waves.
Examples of transverse waves include:
- **Electromagnetic Waves**: Light waves, radio waves, microwaves, and other forms of electromagnetic radiation are transverse waves. In these waves, the electric and magnetic fields oscillate perpendicular to the direction of propagation.
- **Water Waves**: Waves on the surface of water are also transverse waves. As a wave travels across the water, the particles of water move up and down (or side to side) in a direction perpendicular to the direction of wave travel.
- **String Waves**: Waves traveling along a stretched string (such as those produced on a guitar or violin) are transverse waves. The particles of the string oscillate up and down perpendicular to the direction of wave travel.

Longitudinal waves : Longitudinal waves are a type of mechanical wave characterized by the oscillation of particles parallel to the direction of wave propagation.
Examples of longitudinal waves include:
- **Sound Waves**: Sound waves traveling through air, liquids, or solids are longitudinal waves. In these waves, the particles of the medium oscillate back and forth in the direction of the wave's propagation.
- **Seismic Waves**: Earthquakes generate seismic waves that travel through the Earth's interior. P-waves (primary waves) are longitudinal waves, with particle motion parallel to the direction of wave travel.
- **Spring Waves:** Waves traveling along a stretched or compressed spring are also longitudinal waves. As the wave travels along the spring, the coils of the spring compress and expand in the direction of wave propagation.

Compression and Rarefaction:

- Longitudinal waves consist of alternating regions of compression and rarefaction.

• In the **compression** regions, particles are crowded together, leading to an increase in pressure. Conversely, in the **rarefaction** regions, particles are spread apart, resulting in a decrease in pressure.

• The distance between successive compressions or rarefactions is called the wavelength of the wave.

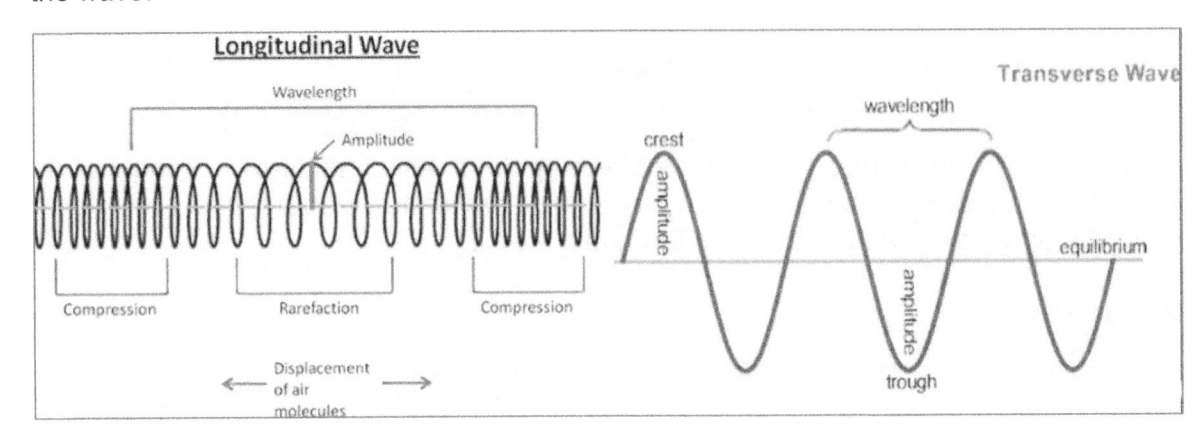

The Doppler effect: The Doppler effect is the change in the observed frequency of a wave when the source or the detector moves relative to the transmitting medium **Behavior of waves is affected by the medium:** The medium a wave travels through affects its behavior. For example, sound waves travel faster in water than in air because water has a higher density. Sound waves travel faster in denser substances because particles bump into each other more easily. A bottle of water has about 800 times more particles than the same bottle of air, so sound waves travel much faster in water.

Chemical Reactions

Chemical elements are substances that consist of only one type of atom. They are the fundamental building blocks of matter and are organized on the periodic table based on their atomic number, which represents the number of protons in the nucleus of each atom.

Here's a brief description of chemical elements:

1. **Atomic Structure**: Each chemical element is characterized by the number of protons in its nucleus, known as the atomic number. Elements may have different numbers of neutrons isotopes), but they all have the same number of protons. The arrangement of electrons around the nucleus determines an element's chemical properties.

2. **Symbol:** Each chemical element is represented by a unique symbol, typically one or two letters derived from its name. For example, hydrogen is represented by the symbol H, oxygen by O, and carbon by C.

3. **Properties**: Chemical elements exhibit a wide range of physical and chemical properties. These properties include characteristics such as color, density, melting point, boiling point, conductivity, reactivity, and abundance in nature.

4. **Classification**: Elements are classified into different categories based on their properties, such as metals, nonmetals, and metalloids. The periodic table organizes elements into groups (columns) and periods (rows) based on similarities in their properties.

5. **Abundance**: Some elements are abundant in nature, while others are relatively rare. Elements like oxygen, silicon, aluminum, and iron are abundant and commonly found in Earth's crust, while elements like gold, platinum, and uranium are less common.

6. **Applications**: Chemical elements are used in various industries and applications. For example, metals like iron, copper, and aluminum are used in construction and manufacturing, while elements like hydrogen and oxygen are essential for life and used in various chemical processes.

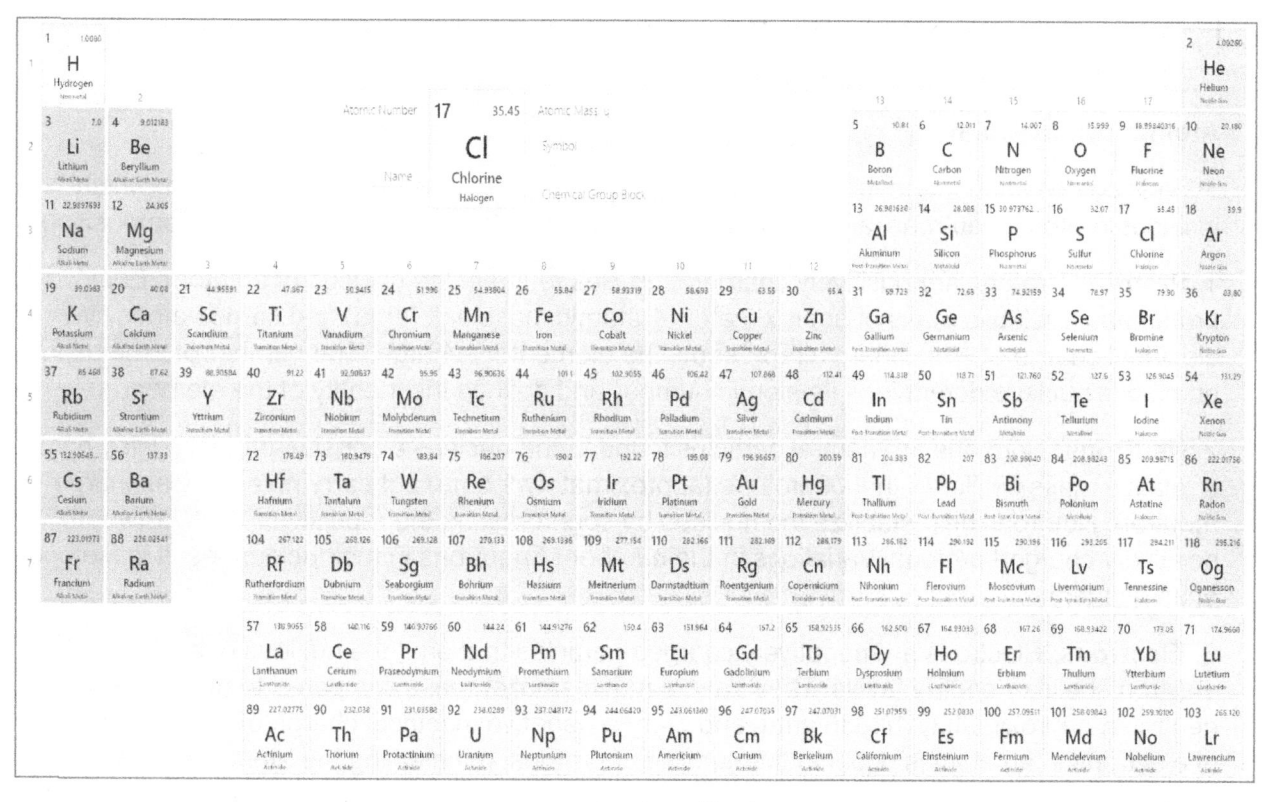

THE COLUMNS ARE GROUPS OR FAMILIES

Periodic Table ☐ Non Metals ☐ Metals ☐ Nobel Gases
☐ Alkali Metals ☐ Metalloids ☐ Rare Earth Met
☐ Alkali Earth ☐ Halogens

Columns = Groups or Families
Rows = Periods

1	2	3	4	5	6	7	8
Alkali Metals	Alkaline Earth	III	Carbon	Nitrogen	Oxygen	Halogens	Nobel Gases
Alkali Metals have one valence electron <u>1VE</u> Highly Reactive Volatile with Water	Alkaline Earth Metals have 2 valence electrons <u>2VE</u> Very Reactive	Group 3 has 3 valence electrons <u>3VE</u>	Group 4 has 4 valence electrons <u>4VE</u>	Group 5 has 5 valence electrons <u>5VE</u>	Group 6 has 6 valence electrons <u>6VE</u>	Halogens have 7 valence electrons <u>7VE</u>	Nobel Gases or Group 8 or 0 are completely stable and need no electrons. Typically these elements do not bond with others.

Reactivity Decreases across the Periodic Table Groups
Density, Boiling, and Melting point increase across the Periodic Table Groups

31

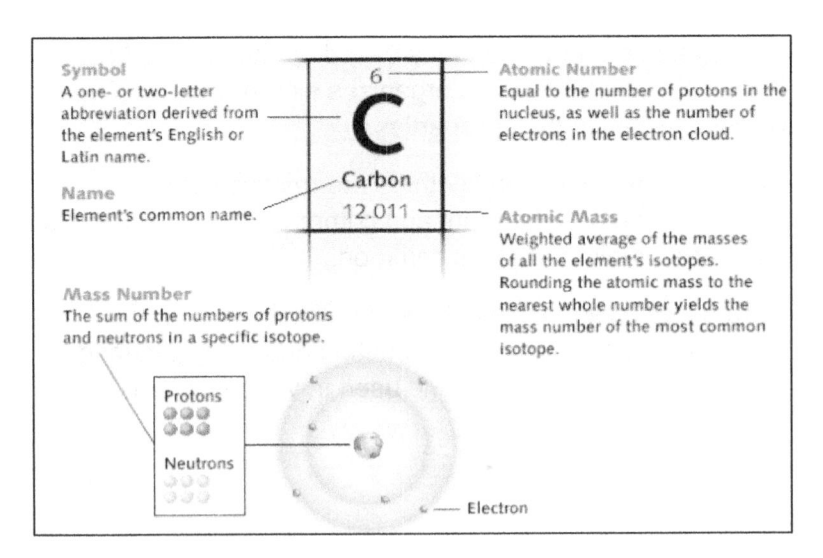

Atomic composition

Atomic composition refers to the arrangement of subatomic particles within an atom, which includes protons, neutrons, and electrons. Here's a brief description of the atomic composition:

1. **Protons**: Protons are positively charged particles found in the nucleus of an atom. Each proton has a relative mass of approximately 1 atomic mass unit (amu) and carries a positive electrical charge of +1e, where e represents the elementary charge. The number of protons in an atom's nucleus determines its atomic number and defines the identity of the element.

2. **Neutrons**: Neutrons are neutral particles found in the nucleus alongside protons. They have a relative mass similar to that of protons (approximately 1 amu) but carry no electrical charge (neutral). Neutrons help stabilize the nucleus by counteracting the repulsive forces between positively charged protons. Variations in the number of neutrons in the nucleus result in isotopes of an element.

3. **Electrons**: Electrons are negatively charged particles that orbit the nucleus of an atom in electron shells or energy levels. They have a much smaller mass compared to protons and neutrons, approximately 1/1836 amu, and carry a negative electrical charge of −1e. The number of electrons in an atom is equal to the number of protons, maintaining the atom's overall neutrality.

The arrangement of protons, neutrons, and electrons within an atom determines its atomic structure and properties. The interactions between these subatomic particles give rise to chemical bonding, chemical reactions, and the behavior of matter at the atomic level. **Chemical elements**

A chemical reaction is a process in which substances, known as reactants, are transformed into different substances, known as products. During a chemical reaction, the atoms in the reactants are rearranged to form new molecules, but the total number of each type of atom remains the same.

Chemical formulas: Identify chemical formulas by ball-and-stick diagram.

Chemical formulas represent the composition of molecules using symbols for the elements and subscripts to indicate the number of atoms of each element present. While ball-and-stick diagrams are typically used to represent molecular structures visually, they can also give an indication of chemical formulas.

Here's how you can identify chemical formulas using a ball-and-stick diagram:

1. **Identify the Elements**: In a ball-and-stick diagram, each ball (or sphere) typically represents an atom, and the sticks (or lines) represent the bonds between atoms. Different colors or sizes of balls may indicate different elements. Identify the elements present in the diagram based on the colors or labels associated with the balls.

2. **Count the Atoms**: Count the number of each type of atom present in the diagram. Each ball representing an atom corresponds to one atom of that element. For example, if you see two red balls in the diagram, it indicates two atoms of the element represented by the color red.

3. **Determine the Chemical Formula**: Once you've identified the elements and counted the number of atoms of each element, you can write the chemical formula using the element symbols and subscripts. The subscript next to each element symbol indicates the number of atoms of that element in the molecule.

4. **Check for Ratios**: Ensure that the subscripts represent the simplest whole number ratio of atoms in the molecule. If necessary, simplify the ratios by dividing all subscripts by the greatest common divisor.

Find the chemical formula for

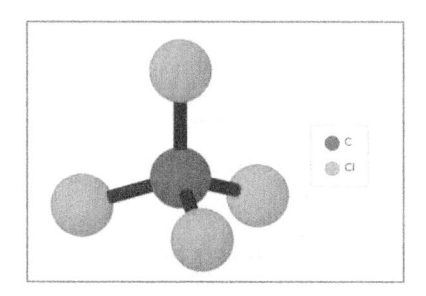

Answer CCl_4

Physical and chemical changes

Physical and chemical changes are two types of transformations that matter can undergo. These changes alter the properties of substances but differ in the way they affect the composition of matter.

Physical Changes:

- Physical changes are alterations in the state or appearance of a substance without changing its chemical composition.
- These changes typically involve a rearrangement of molecules or particles but do not result in the formation of new substances.
- Examples of physical changes include changes in state (such as melting, freezing, vaporization, and condensation), changes in shape or size (such as cutting, crushing, or dissolving), and changes in physical properties (such as changes in color, density, or texture).

- Physical changes are usually **reversible**, meaning the original substance can be recovered without altering its chemical identity.
- Energy may be absorbed or released during physical changes, but there is no net gain or loss of energy.

Chemical Changes:

- Chemical changes, also known as chemical reactions, involve the breaking and forming of chemical bonds, resulting in the formation of new substances with different chemical compositions.
- Chemical changes often involve the exchange, rearrangement, or combination of atoms to form new molecules or compounds.
- Examples of chemical changes include combustion (burning), rusting of iron, fermentation of food, digestion of food in the body, and photosynthesis in plants.
- Chemical changes are typically accompanied by observable signs, such as the release of heat or light, color change, formation of a precipitate, or production of gas.
- Unlike physical changes, chemical changes are usually irreversible, meaning the original substances cannot be recovered through simple physical means.
- Chemical reactions involve the transfer or transformation of energy, which can be in the form of heat, light, or electricity.

Count atoms and molecules in chemical reactions

Here's a step-by-step approach to counting atoms and molecules in chemical reactions:

1. **Write the Balanced Chemical Equation**: Start by writing the balanced chemical equation for the reaction. A balanced equation ensures that the number of atoms of each element is the same on both sides of the reaction arrow.

2. **Identify Reactants and Products**: Determine the substances that are reacting (reactants) and those that are formed (products) in the chemical reaction.

3. **Count Atoms in Reactants**: For each element present in the reactants, count the number of atoms based on the coefficients (numbers in front of the chemical formulas) in the balanced equation. Multiply the coefficient by the subscript of each element in the formula to find the total number of atoms of that element.

4. **Count Atoms in Products:** Repeat the process for the products of the reaction, counting the number of atoms of each element based on the coefficients in the balanced equation.

5. **Check for Conservation of Mass**: Ensure that the total number of atoms of each element is the same on both sides of the balanced equation. Conservation of mass dictates that matter cannot be created or destroyed in a chemical reaction, so the number of atoms of each element must be equal on both sides.

6. **Adjust Coefficients if Necessary**: If the equation is not balanced, adjust the coefficients of the reactants and/or products to achieve balance. Ensure that the same number of each type of atom is present on both sides of the equation.

7. **Consider Stoichiometric Ratios**: Use the coefficients in the balanced equation to determine the mole ratios between reactants and products. This information can be used to calculate quantities of reactants consumed or products formed in the reaction.

Calculate amounts of reactants or products in chemical reactions

To calculate the amounts of reactants or products in a chemical reaction, you typically follow these steps:

1. **Write the Balanced Chemical Equation**: Start by writing the balanced chemical equation for the reaction. This equation shows the reactants on the left side and the products on the right side, with the same number of atoms of each element on both sides.

2. **Convert Given Amounts to Moles**: If you're given the amounts of reactants or products in grams, convert these amounts to moles using the molar mass of each substance. You can find the molar mass by adding up the atomic masses of all the atoms in the chemical formula.

3. **Use Stoichiometry**: Use the coefficients in the balanced equation to set up mole ratios between the substances involved in the reaction. This allows you to relate the amounts of reactants to the amounts of products.

4. **Calculate**: Multiply the moles of the given substance by the appropriate mole ratio to find the moles of the desired substance.

5. **Convert Back to Desired Units**: If necessary, convert the moles of the desired substance back to the units you need (grams, liters, etc.) using the appropriate conversion factors.

6. **Check Units and Sig Figs**: Make sure your final answer has the correct units and the appropriate number of significant figures.

Here's an example: Consider the reaction between hydrogen gas (H_2) and oxygen gas (O_2) to form water (H_2O).

Balanced equation: $2 H_2(g) + O_2(g) \rightarrow 2 H_2O(g)$

Let's say you have 5.00 grams of hydrogen gas (H_2) and you want to know how much water (H_2O) can be produced.

1. Convert the given mass of hydrogen gas to moles using its molar mass.
   Molar mass of H_2 = 2.02 g/mol Moles of H_2 = 5.00 g / 2.02 g/mol = 2.48 mol (rounded to 3 significant figures)
2. Use the mole ratio from the balanced equation to find the moles of water produced.
   From the balanced equation, the mole ratio of H_2 to H_2O is 2:2. Moles of H_2O produced = (2.48 mol H_2) × (2 mol H_2O / 2 mol H_2) = 2.48 mol H_2O
3. Convert the moles of water to grams using the molar mass of water.
   Molar mass of H_2O = 18.02 g/mol Mass of H_2O produced = (2.48 mol H_2O) × (18.02 g/mol) = 44.7 g (rounded to 3 significant figures)

   So, 5.00 grams of hydrogen gas will produce approximately 44.7 grams of water.

Chapter 4: Life Sciences

Life science, also known as **biology**, is the study of living things and the processes that govern their existence.
Life science encompasses a wide range of topics, including the diversity of life, the structure and function of organisms, ecosystems and environmental interactions, heredity and genetics, and human biology.

Key Concepts covered in this section are:

Ecosystems	Ecosystems are dynamic communities of living organisms interacting with each other and their environment. Students will learn about the flow of energy through ecosystems, the cycling of nutrients, and the importance of biodiversity.
Structure and function of organisms	Organisms exhibit diverse structures and functions that enable them to survive and thrive in their environments. Students will explore the hierarchical organization of living things, from cells to organ systems and plant processes
Heredity	Heredity is the transmission of genetic information from parents to offspring. Students will delve into the principles of inheritance, genetic variation, and the role of genetics in shaping traits.

Ecosystems: Interactions, energy flow, and biodiversity

Ecosystems are complex networks of living organisms and their physical environment, where interactions occur among various species and elements. In Life Science, students explore the dynamics of ecosystems, including the flow of energy, the cycling of matter, and the importance of biodiversity. This section introduces students to the key components of ecosystems and the intricate relationships that sustain life within them.

Ecosystem Components:

- Ecosystems consist of biotic (living) and abiotic (non-living) components. Biotic components include plants, animals, fungi, and microorganisms, while abiotic components include sunlight, water, soil, air, and temperature.
- Each organism occupies a specific niche within the ecosystem, fulfilling unique roles in energy transfer, nutrient cycling, and habitat maintenance.

Energy Flow:

- Energy flows through ecosystems in a unidirectional manner, primarily driven by the sun. **Producers**, such as plants and algae, harness sunlight to convert solar energy into chemical energy through photosynthesis.
- **Consumers**, including herbivores, carnivores, omnivores, and decomposers, obtain energy by consuming other organisms and breaking down organic matter.

Nutrient Cycling:

- Nutrients, such as carbon, nitrogen, and phosphorus, cycle through ecosystems in biogeochemical cycles. These cycles involve the movement of nutrients between living organisms, soil, water, and the atmosphere.
- **Decomposers** play a vital role in nutrient cycling by breaking down dead organic matter and returning nutrients to the soil for reuse by plants.

Biodiversity:

- Biodiversity refers to the variety of species and genetic diversity within an ecosystem. High levels of biodiversity contribute to ecosystem resilience, stability, and productivity.
- Ecosystems with greater biodiversity are better able to withstand environmental disturbances, adapt to changing conditions, and support a wide range of ecological functions and services.

Food webs and food chains

Food chain a sequence of connected producers and consumers. Energy is transferred to higher levels in the food chain.

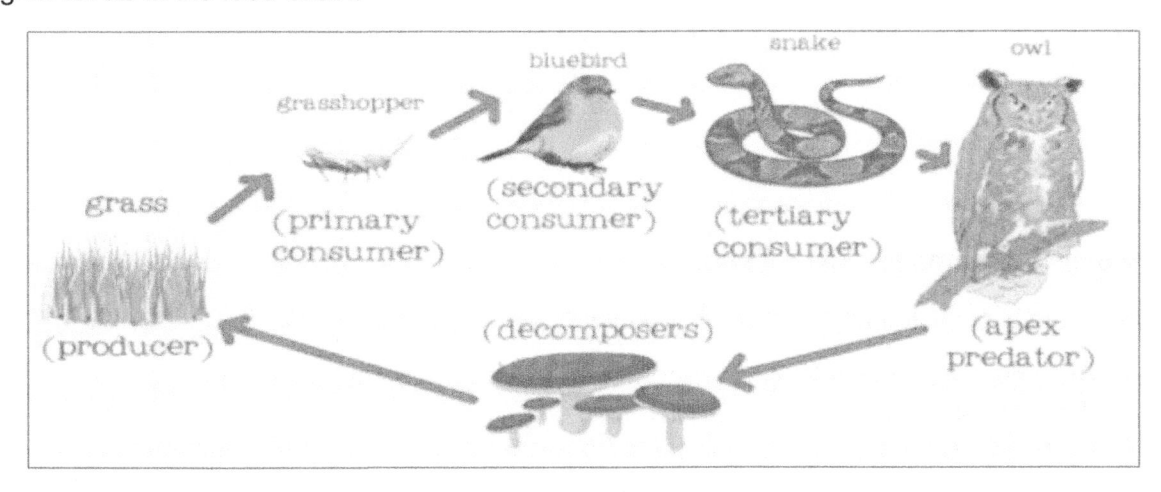

Food web interrelated food chains that interact within an ecosystem. A food web shows the interdependence of organisms in an ecosystem

- Plants use energy from light to make sugar (glucose) from carbon dioxide. This is known as **photosynthesis**.
- Plants (producers)can use the food they make immediately or they can store the food. Green plants can make food for themselves directly (photosynthesis) or indirectly for consumers
- Energy flows through the ecosystem from the **Sun → Producers → Consumers**.
- **Decomposers** gather their energy from producers and consumers, often after death occurs. They return nutrients to the environment.
- Fungi are a type of decomposer. Besides breaking down dead plants and animal matter, fungi can also break down pollution in the soil.
- Bacteria can also serve as decomposers. Nitrogen-fixing bacteria help move nitrogen through the ecosystem.
- Water, carbon dioxide, nitrogen and oxygen cycled between living and nonliving.

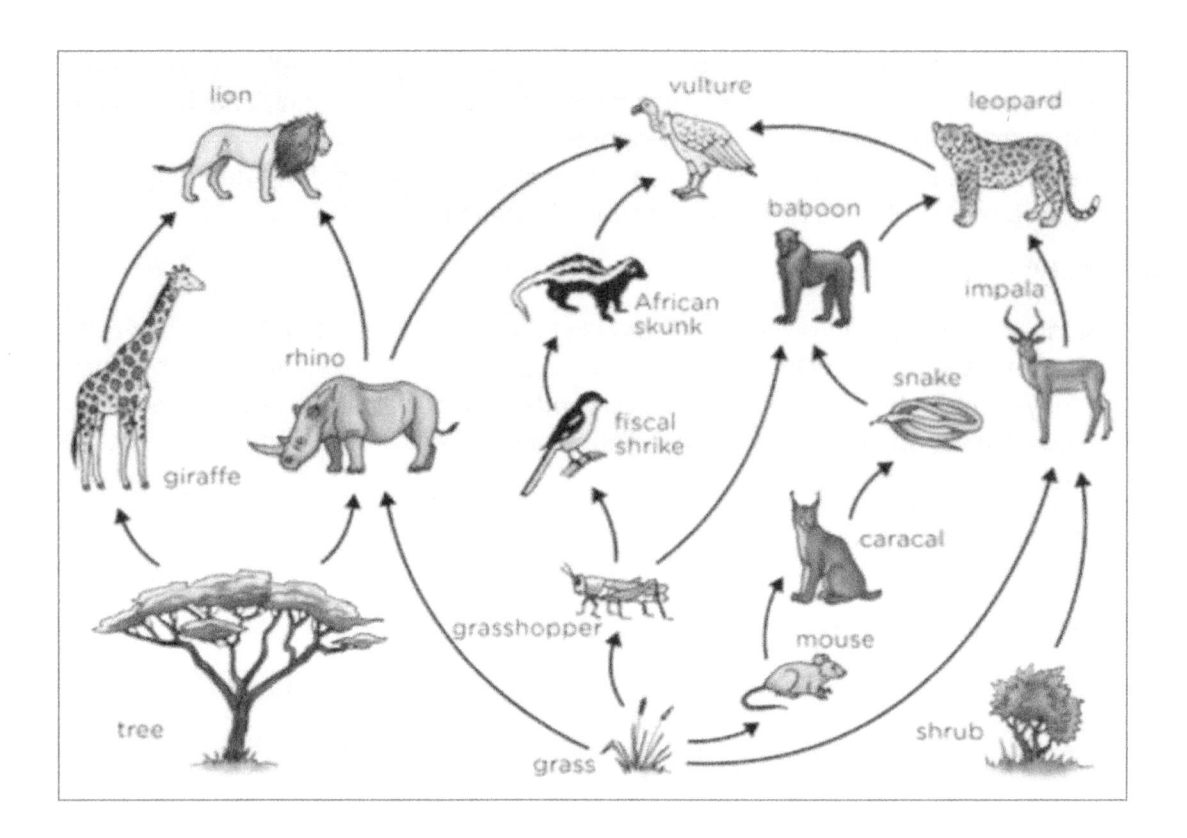

How plants respond to external stimuli

Environmental conditions can affect the survival of individual organisms.

- **Dormancy** is a period of inactivity where mature seeds remain dormant (slows down, stops) until conditions are favorable for germination or growth.
- **Germination** is the development of plant from a seed or a spore. Plants have the ability to grow, reproduce, shift the position of their roots or leaves in response to environmental conditions such as gravity, sunlight, temperature and day length
- **Tropism** is a plant turning or bending movement toward or away from heat, light and gravity. Positive tropism - plant grows TOWARDS the stimuli. For example, a stem grows to the light Negative tropism - plant grows AWAY from the stimuli. For example, roots grow away from the light

To survive, organisms must be able to withstand abiotic and biotic changes in their environment

A limiting factor is any biotic or abiotic factor that restricts the existence, number, reproduction, or distribution of organisms

- Can be abiotic (non-living) such as water, light, temperature, atmosphere and soil
- Can be biotic (living or once living) such as species, populations, communities

The Theory of Evolution

"All living species are descendants of ancestral species and are different from present day ones due to the cumulative change in the genetic composition of a population"

Descent with Modification: – All organisms on Earth are related through some unknown ancestral type that lived long ago.

The Six Main Points of Darwin's Theory of Evolution

1. **Overproduction** • Most species produce far more offspring than are needed to maintain the population. • Species populations remain more or less constant ("stable") because a small fraction of offspring live long enough to reproduce
2. **Competition** • Living space and food are limited, so offspring from each generation must compete among themselves in order to live. • Only a small fraction can possibly survive long enough to reproduce.
3. **Genetic Variation** • Characteristics in individuals in any species are not exactly alike. – Ex: Differences for Homo sapiens (humans) can be exact size or shape of body, strength in running, or resistance to disease. • These differences are considered to be the variations within a species. What causes slight variations between individuals?
4. **Adaptation:** An adaptation is an inherited trait that increases an organisms' chance of survival and reproduction in a given environment.
5. **Natural Selection** • Nature/environment selects for living organisms with better suited inherited traits to survive and reproduce. • Offspring inherit these better traits, and as a whole the population improves for that particular environment. Natural Selection does not move in a predetermined direction! The changing earth determines what will and can survive.
6. **Speciation** • Over many generations, favorable adaptations (in a particular environment) gradually accumulate in a species and "bad" ones (in a particular environment) disappear. • Eventually, accumulated changes become so great, the result is a new species. • Formation of a new species is called "Speciation" and it takes many, many generations to do.

Evidence of Evolution

1. Fossil Evidence

- Carbon dating--gives an age of a sample based on the amount of radioactive carbon is in a sample.
- **Fossil record**---creates a geologic time scale.
- Fossils reveal existence of transitional species

2. Homologous Structures-

- -structures that are embryologically similar, but have different functions, the wing of a bird and the forearm of a human

3. Vestigial Structures

- Organs or parts that have no current function
- Examples include pelvic bones in whales

4. Biochemistry and DNA

- DNA of closely related species have similar sequences
- Proteins and other biochemicals are similar across related species (Cytochrome C)

5. Embryological development

- Embryos follow similar patterns of development
- Early embryos of different species look very similar

6. Direct Observation

- Antibiotic resistance in bacteria
- Rock Pocket mice coloration
- Tuskless elephants

Structure and Function of Organisms

The structure and function of organisms are fundamental concepts in life science that help us understand how living things are adapted to their environments and how they carry out essential life processes.

Structural Adaptations:

Structural adaptations refer to physical features or characteristics that enable organisms to survive and thrive in their environments. These adaptations may include:

- Body shape and size
- Skeletal structures and support systems
- Protective coverings, such as shells, feathers, or fur
- Specialized appendages, organs, or tissues for specific functions

Functional Adaptations:

Functional adaptations involve physiological, biochemical, or behavioral traits that enhance an organism's ability to perform essential life functions. These adaptations may include:

- Sensory systems for detecting stimuli, such as sight, hearing, smell, taste, and touch
- Digestive systems for obtaining and processing nutrients from food
- Respiratory systems for exchanging gases, such as oxygen and carbon dioxide
- Circulatory systems for transporting nutrients, oxygen, and waste products throughout the body

Relationship Between Structure and Function:

- The structure of an organism is closely related to its function. Organisms are adapted to perform specific functions based on their unique structural features.
- For example, the long, thin shape of a bird's beak is adapted for probing into flowers to extract nectar or catching insects for food. The structure of the beak is directly related to its function in obtaining food.

Living organisms: Plants and animals

By observing their properties (characteristics that describe an object), scientists have divided all things into two groups: living and non-living. All living things, known as **organisms**, must have the following characteristics.

- be made up of one or more cells.
- need and use energy to carry out life activities.
- use food and excrete waste.
- be adapted (suited) to their environment (surroundings).
- respond to changes in their environment.
- reproduce organisms like themselves.
- grow and develop.

Cells

Cells, the "building blocks of life," are the smallest living things. All organisms are made up of cells. Some living things are **unicellular** and carry out all the basic life activities within that single cell. however, most living things are **multicellular**.

Cell Theory

- All organisms are made up of one or many cells.
- Cells are the basic unit of structure and function in all organisms.
- All cells come from other cells that already exist

Cells: Structure and parts

Cells : Cells are the structural, functional and biological units of all living beings. A cell can replicate itself independently. Hence, they are known as building blocks of life. All organisms are made up of cells.

Cell Structure:

The cell structure comprises individual components with specific functions essential to carry out life's processes. These components includes :

Cell Membrane (Plasma Membrane): The Cell membrane is the selectively permeable outer boundary of the cell. Selective permeability means to regulate and allow only selected substances to move in and out of the cell. Consists of lipids and proteins.

Cytoplasm: It is a jelly-like substance that provides a surface for all the organelles in the cell. Cytoplasm is made up of water, salts, and other organic molecules.

Nucleus: The Nucleus is called the 'control center' of the cell as it regulates all the functions of the cell. It is just like the brain of the human body. It also has different parts with different functions.

- **Nuclear Envelope**: • It is a double membrane surrounding the nucleus. • Contains pores for the exchange of materials between the nucleus and cytoplasm.
- **Nucleolus**: • A dense structure inside the nucleus. • Involved in the production of ribosomes.
- Chromatin Network It is a tangled fibrous body inside the nucleus. Ot contains our genetic material, DNA (Deoxyribonucleic acid)
- **Nucleoplasm** It is a gel-like substance inside the nucleus Endoplasmic Reticulum (ER): • It is a network of membrane-bound tubes and sacs. • Rough ER has ribosomes attached and is involved in protein synthesis. • Smooth ER is involved in lipid synthesis and detoxification. Liver cells generally have a lot of smooth ER • The process of synthesizing the cell membrane from proteins from Rough ER and Lipids in Smooth ER

Ribosomes: They are small structures produced by nucleus which are composed of RNA (Ribonucleic acid) and protein. • Site of protein synthesis.

Golgi Apparatus (Golgi Body): • Stack of flattened membrane sacs (cisternae). • Modifies, sorts, and packages proteins for secretion or transport. • Discovered by Camilio Golgi

Mitochondria: • It is commonly known as the powerhouse of the cell. • Site of cellular respiration, where ATP (energy) is generated. • It is a semi-autonomous organelle, meaning that it contains its own DNA and ribosomes.

Chloroplasts (in plant cells): • Found in plant cells and some algae. • Site of photosynthesis, where light energy is converted into chemical energy (glucose). • Contains chlorophyll, a pigment that captures light energy.

Vacuoles: • Membrane-bound sacs for storage of water, nutrients, or waste products. • Larger and more prominent in plant cells while small and temporary in animally

Lysosomes (in animal cells): • Membrane-bound organelles containing digestive enzymes. • Break down macromolecules and recycle cellular waste. • Known as the suicide bags of the cell because they burst when cell gets damaged heavily, the digestive enzymes of the lysosomes digest their own cell

Cytoskeleton: • Network of protein filaments (microfilaments, intermediate filaments, microtubules). • Provides structural support, facilitates cell movement, and helps in intracellular transport.

Understanding the structure and function of these cellular components is important for comprehending how cells operate and interact within organisms.

Plant Cell and Animal Cell : A plant cell has some organelles which distinguish it from an animal cell. They are:

- Cell Wall, which is the protective hard outer cover of the cell.
- Plastids, which make the food for the cells.

- Vacuole, which is used for storage and covers a large portion of the cell

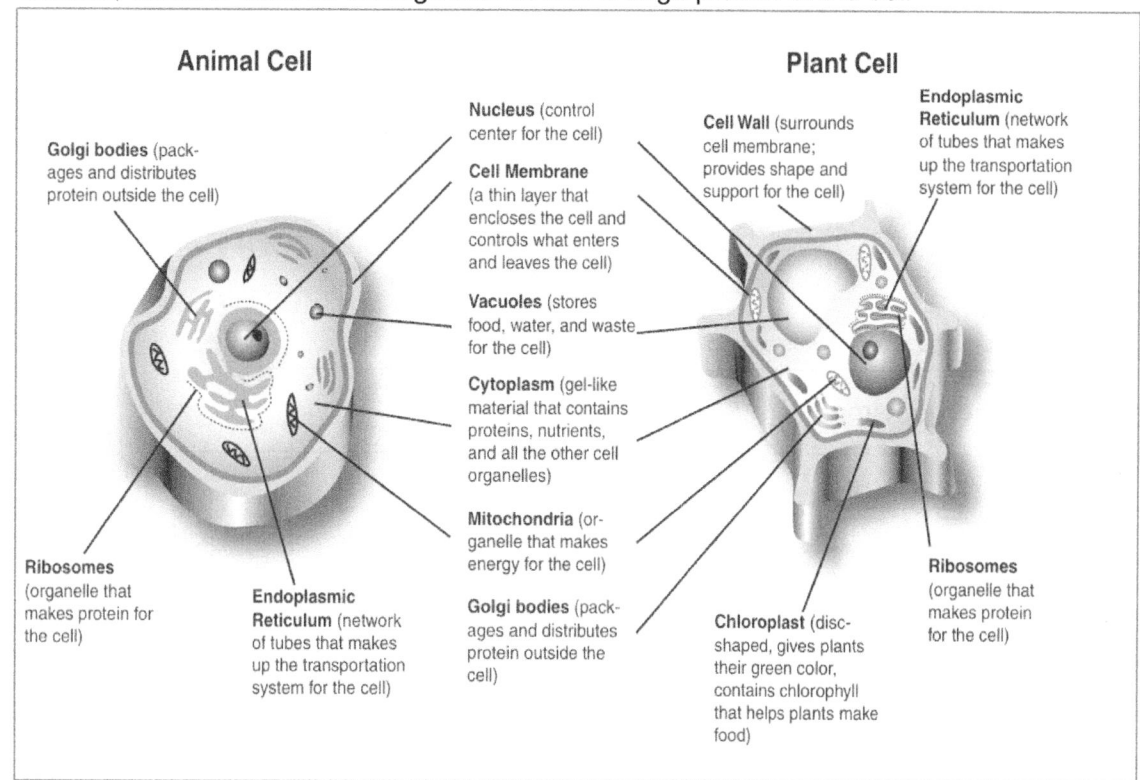

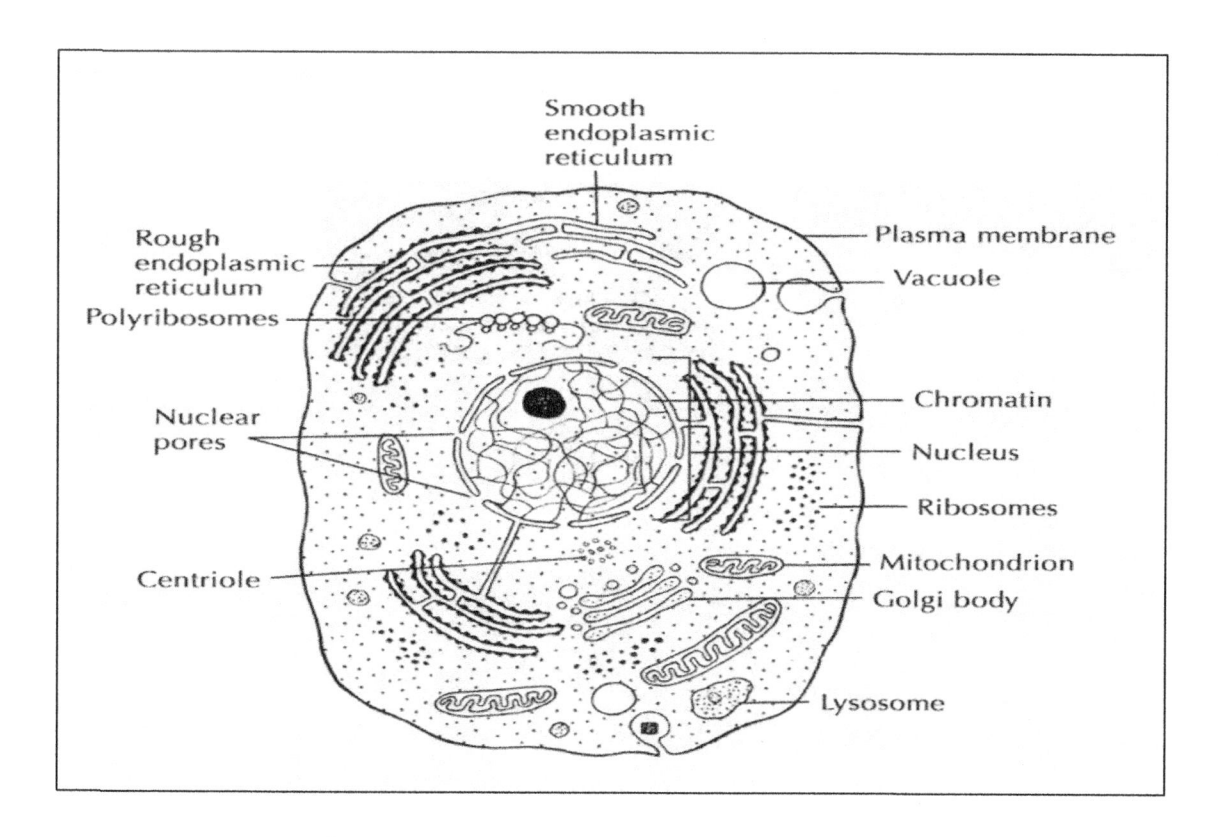

Animal Cell

Golgi bodies (packages and distributes protein outside the cell)

Nucleus (control center for the cell)

Cell Membrane (a thin layer that encloses the cell and controls what enters and leaves the cell)

Vacuoles (stores food, water, and waste for the cell)

Cytoplasm (gel-like material that contains proteins, nutrients, and all the other cell organelles)

Mitochondria (organelle that makes energy for the cell)

Golgi bodies (packages and distributes protein outside the cell)

Ribosomes (organelle that makes protein for the cell)

Endoplasmic Reticulum (network of tubes that makes up the transportation system for the cell)

Plant Cell

Cell Wall (surrounds cell membrane; provides shape and support for the cell)

Endoplasmic Reticulum (network of tubes that makes up the transportation system for the cell)

Ribosomes (organelle that makes protein for the cell)

Chloroplast (disc-shaped, gives plants their green color, contains chlorophyll that helps plants make food)

Labels on animal cell diagram:
- Smooth endoplasmic reticulum
- Rough endoplasmic reticulum
- Polyribosomes
- Nuclear pores
- Centriole
- Plasma membrane
- Vacuole
- Chromatin
- Nucleus
- Ribosomes
- Mitochondrion
- Golgi body
- Lysosome

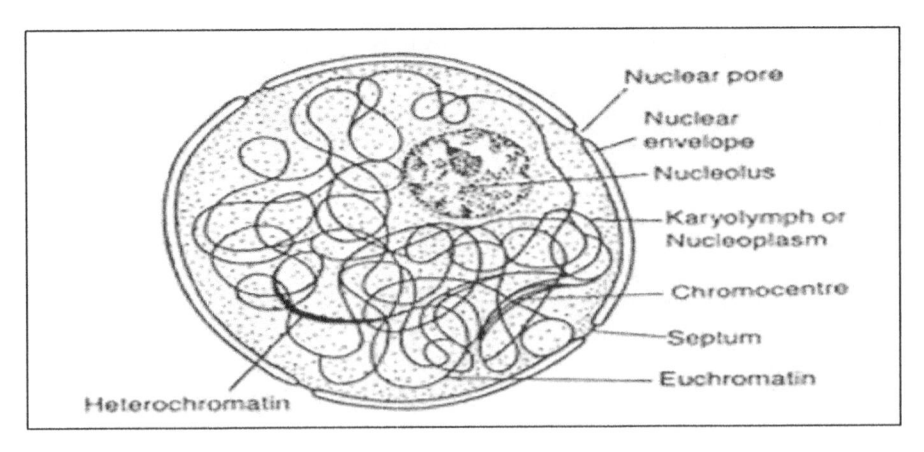

Unicellular organisms:

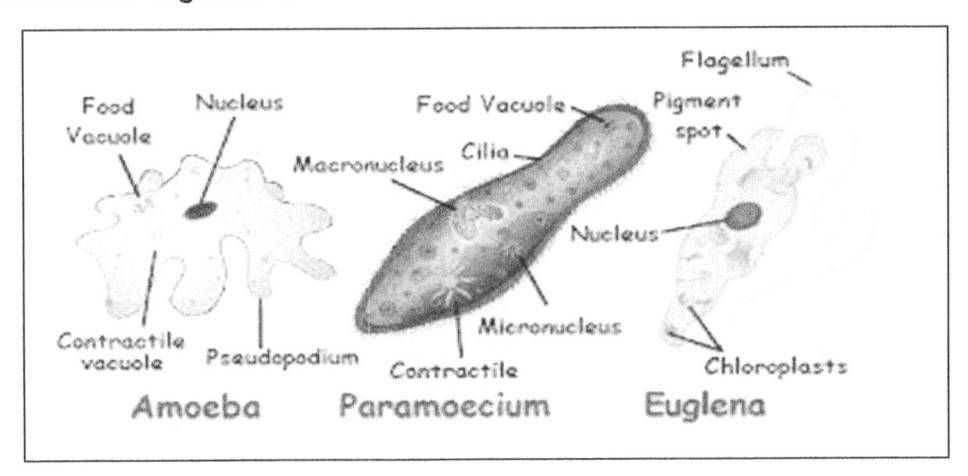

Multicellular organisms:

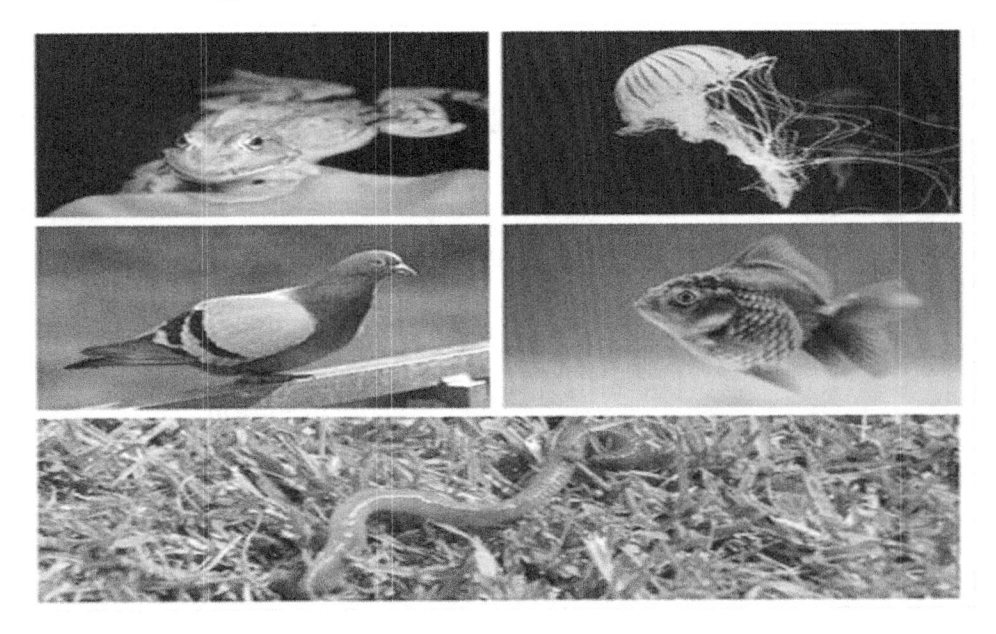

Cell Diffusion and Osmosis The cell's membrane controls what enters and leaves a cell. To carry on life processes, oxygen, food, and water must pass through the cell's membrane, and

44

waste products must be removed from the cell through the membrane. The membrane has tiny holes in it.

Molecules (very small substances) can go in and out by moving through the tiny holes.

Diffusion (the movement of molecules into and out of the cell) helps the cell carry out all the basic life activities.

Cells contain water and are surrounded by water. A cell needs water to maintain a constant temperature, shape, and size for life processes to occur. **Osmosis** (movement of water molecules into and out of a cell) is a special kind of cell diffusion.

Plants Structure and Processes:

Plants are multicellular organisms. Plants make their own food in a process called photosynthesis. Because plants can make their own food, scientists classify them as producers. Plants can be divided into two major groups:

vascular (having tube-like structures inside the plant to carry food, water, and minerals) and **nonvascular** (no tube-like structures to carry food and water through the plant).

Vascular plants do not need as much direct contact with water. As a result, they are able to grow in almost every kind of environment. Vascular plants produce leaves, stems, and roots. The leaves make food for the plant with the help of sunlight and chlorophyll. The **xylem** (water transporting tissues) and **phloem** (tissue responsible for moving food down from the leaves to other parts of the plant) carry water to the leaves and food to all parts of the plant. They include plants such as maple trees, tomatoes, and roses. **nonvascular plants** do not have leaves, stems, or roots. Most nonvascular plants are found in moist areas. They include mosses, hornworts, and liverworts.

The process of photosynthesis

Photosynthesis (the process plants use to make food) happens in the leaf. The green leaves absorb light energy from the sun. They also take in carbon dioxide from the air through the **stomata** (tiny openings in the leaves). Water and minerals from the soil travel through the roots and stems of the plant to combine with **chlorophyll** (the green chemical in the leaf that allows plants to trap the sun's energy), sunlight, and carbon dioxide to produce glucose (sugar). Glucose is the usable food for green plants.

Respiration, the exchange of gases and water between plants and the atmosphere, is a continuous cycle. Respiration is important to the process of making glucose. The plant takes in carbon dioxide and gives off oxygen through the stomata during photosynthesis. During **transpiration** (evaporation of water from a plant) the water the plant does not need for photosynthesis is released into the atmosphere through the stomata.

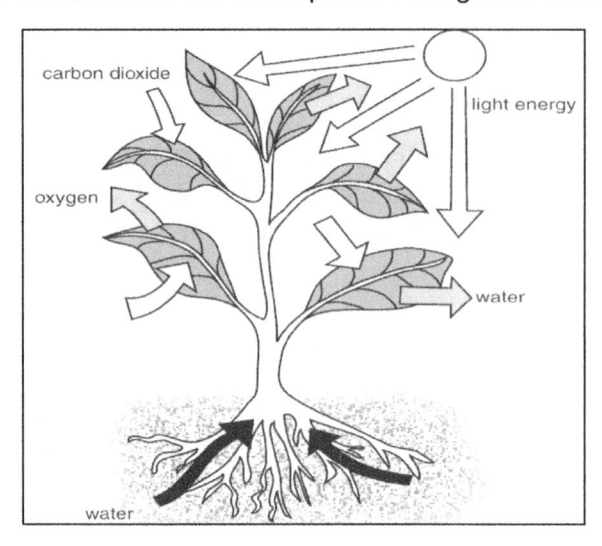

How Plants Reproduce

Method of Reproduction	Examples
sexual: joining two cells, male cell and female cell, making a new organism in a process called fertilization	- flowers - cones - spores
asexual: reproduction that does not involve male and female cells combining	- budding - eyes - runners - bulbs

Classification	Type of Seed	Examples
Angiosperms: flowering plants	- seeds are surrounded by the tissues that eventually become fruits	- maple trees - daises
Gymnosperms: nonflowering plants	- produce seeds inside cones - spores	- fir trees, spruce - ferns, mosses

Flowering Plants

Flowers perform the job of reproduction for the plant. The **pistil** (female reproductive part of the flower) consists of the stigma, style, ovary, and egg cells. The **stamen** (male reproductive part of a flower) contains the anther, filament, and pollen (sperm cells).

Pollination (the movement of pollen from one plant to another) is necessary for seeds to form in flowering plants. The stamen is the male reproductive part of a flower.

The stamen consists of two parts: the **filament** and the **anther**.

Some flowers are **self-pollinators** (have everything they need to pollinate in just one plant). The pollen grains will travel from the stamens of the plant to the pistil of the same plant. other flowers are cross pollinators (need another plant to make the pollination complete). **Cross pollinators** often have large colorful blooms. They may have a sweet scent and sweeter nectar. They attract insects and birds to their flowers. These animals pick up the pollen grains while feeding and carry them to another flower. Flowers become fruit after pollination. Fruit provides a covering for seeds. Fruit can be fleshy like an apple or hard like a nut

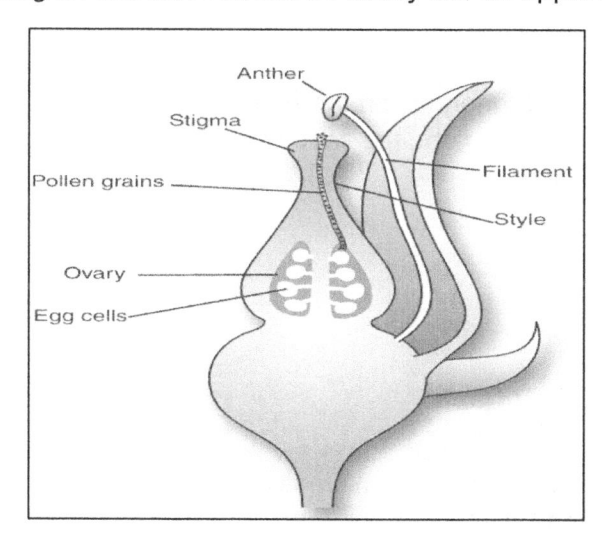

Seeds

In flowering plants, seeds form in the fruit. Seeds have three parts: seed coat (protects new plant inside seed), embryo (new plant), and the cotyledon (seed leaves). Most seeds are monocots (having one cotyledon) or dicots (having two cotyledons)

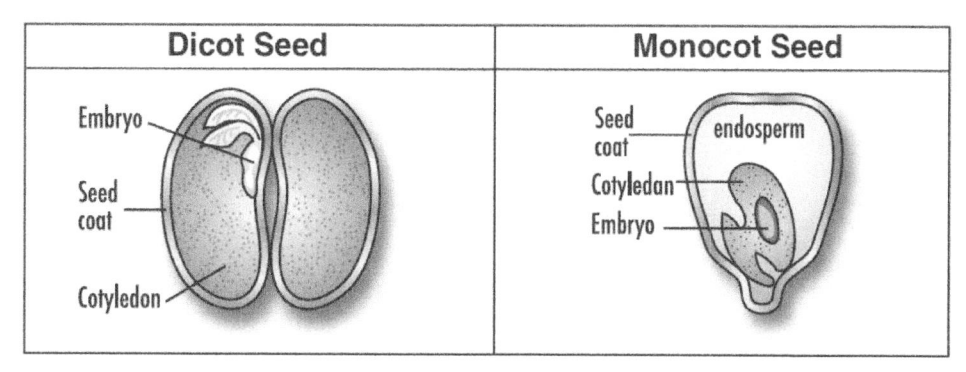

Characteristic	Dicot	Monocot
flower	- four or five petals or multiples of four or five	- three petals or multiples of three
leaves	- branching veins	- parallel veins
roots	- taproot	- fibrous

Germination (early growth of a plant from a seed) depends on three factors: temperature, moisture, and oxygen. When the three conditions are right, the seed opens, and the embryo emerges.

Animal Kingdom:

The animal kingdom, while diverse, can be divided into two main categories. These categories encompass all animals. They are **invertebrates** (animals without backbones) and **vertebrates** (animals with backbones). Within the categories of vertebrate and invertebrate, there are several subcategories that further classify the animals

Invertebrates make up a large part of the animal kingdom. They can live on land, or they can live in the water. Invertebrates are subdivided by their structure and form.

| Invertebrates ||
Types	Characteristics
Sponges	- simplest invertebrate - body two layers of cells thick - simple supporting structure - hollow tube-shaped body with opening at the top
Hollow-bodies	- opening at top of tube-shaped body surrounded by tentacles - tentacles grasp food and bring to mouth - tentacles used for defense
Worms	- simple digestive systems - simple brain - smell receptors - ear spots - sense of touch - sense of taste - includes flatworms, roundworms, and segmented worms
Mollusks	- live in water or wet areas - some have soft bodies - some have protective shells - lack segments and legs
Arthropods	- divided bodies; each segment has a specific function - jointed legs - **exoskeleton** (hard outer shell that protects the body)
Echinoderms	- spiny-skinned - marine animals - central body - arms in multiples of five - supporting skeletal structure just under skin

| vertebrates ||
Types	Characteristics
Fish	- gills - lay eggs - **cold-blooded** (body temperature that changes with the temperature of its surroundings)
Amphibians	- most young have gills - most adults have lungs - lay eggs in water or moist ground - cold-blooded
Reptiles	- dry scaly skin - eggs have tough skin - cold blooded
Birds	- have feathers - have wings - lay eggs - **warm-blooded** (constant body temperature)
Mammals	- hair at some point in life - young drink mother's milk - warm-blooded

Human Body Systems

1. **Skeletal System** - It supports the overall structure of the body and protects the organs.
2. **Muscular System** - The muscular system works closely with the skeletal system. Muscles help the body to move and interact with the world.
3. **Circulatory system** - Transports blood along with nutrients, oxygen to different parts of the body.
4. **Digestive System** - It helps to convert food into nutrients and energy for the body.
5. **Nervous System** - It helps the body to communicate and allows the brain to control various functions of the body.
6. **Respiratory System** – It brings oxygen into the body through the lungs and windpipe. It also removes carbon dioxide from the body.

7. **Endocrine System** - It produces hormones that help regulate the other systems in the body.
8. **Excretory System**– It eliminates the waste metabolic products from the body.
9. **Immune System** - The lymphatic and immune systems work together to protect the body from diseases.
10. **Reproductive System** - The reproductive system includes the sex organs that enable people to have babies. This system is different for males and females.
11. **Skeletal System**
    - Bones– Provide structural framework.
    - Joints -Place where two or more bones connect.
    - Cartilage -It is a soft, gel-like padding between bones that protects joints and facilitates movement.
    - Ligaments - It is an elastic band of tissue that connects bone to bone and provides stability to the joint.

Perception and Motion

• **Components**: Sensory organs (eyes, ears, nose, tongue, skin), musculoskeletal system (muscles, bones, joints). enables movement and coordination.

• **Function**: Perceives and interprets sensory information from the environment,

• **Key Processes**: Eyes perceive light, ears perceive sound, nose perceives smells, tongue perceives taste, skin perceives touch, muscles contract and relax to produce movement.

Heredity

Scientists studied cells for many years before they discovered how **traits** (characteristics) of the parents were passed on to their offspring. By the end of the nineteenth century, scientists had learned the secret code of **heredity** (passing physical and character traits from one generation to another). **Chromosomes** (rod-shaped strands containing genetic material) located in the nucleus of the cell are made up of genes. The genes consisted of a long strand of **DNA**. The DNA contains the genetic blueprint (code) for how an organism looks and functions. The substances in the DNA are arranged in a three-dimensional structure that looks like a ladder. During cell division, the ladder unzips and gives each new cell a copy of the genetic information

Key terms:

Genotype: The genotype refers to the genetic makeup of an organism. It represents the specific combination of alleles (alternative forms of a gene) that an individual possesses for a particular trait. Genotypes are typically represented by letters or symbols that denote the alleles present at specific gene loci. For example, in humans, the genotype for blood type can be represented as AA, AO, BB, BO, AB, or OO, where A and B are alleles for the ABO blood group system.

Genotypes can be homozygous (having two identical alleles for a gene) or heterozygous (having two different alleles for a gene).

Phenotype: The phenotype refers to the observable traits or characteristics of an organism, which are determined by its genotype as well as environmental influences. Phenotypes can include physical features (such as eye color, height, and shape), biochemical traits (such as enzyme activity and blood type), and behavioral characteristics (such as temperament and intelligence). While the genotype provides the genetic instructions for trait development, the phenotype represents the expression of those instructions in the observable characteristics of the organism. Phenotypes can vary widely within a population due to genetic variation, environmental factors, and interactions between genes and the environment.

Dominant: A dominant allele is one that is expressed and masks the effect of the recessive allele when present in the genotype. In a heterozygous individual (one with two different alleles for a particular gene), the dominant allele determines the phenotype, meaning the trait associated with the dominant allele is expressed. Dominant alleles are typically represented by uppercase letters in genetic notation.

Recessive: • A recessive allele is one that is expressed only when two copies of it are present in the genotype (homozygous recessive). In a heterozygous individual, the recessive allele is not expressed phenotypically because its effect is masked by the dominant allele. Recessive alleles are only expressed phenotypically in the absence of the dominant allele. Recessive alleles are typically represented by lowercase letters in genetic notation.

The characteristics of all living things are called **traits**.

Every living thing is a collection of **inherited traits** (characteristics passed down to an individual by his or her parents). These traits are controlled by genes made up of DNA and located on the chromosomes. Traits are passed on to new cells during meiosis.

Gregor Mendel was the first person to describe how traits are inherited. his studies of the inherited traits of pea plants led to the **Laws of Dominance** (principles of genetics). he noticed that genes always came in pairs. Every organism that reproduces sexually receives two genes for every trait. A trait may be **dominant** (stronger), and that trait will show up in the organism. If a trait is **recessive** (weaker), it will not show up in the organism unless the organism inherits two recessive genes.

Punnett squares.

Punnett squares are a simple graphical tool used to predict the possible outcomes of a genetic cross between two individuals. They help determine the probability of offspring inheriting specific alleles for a particular trait.

The Punnett square consists of four boxes inside a square. Each box represents a possible gene combination. The parents' genes are placed outside the square Example: This Punnett square shows the cross between two tall pea plants. Each one has one tall gene and one short gene. T = Tall gene (dominate trait) and t = short gene (recessive trait).

Punnett Square

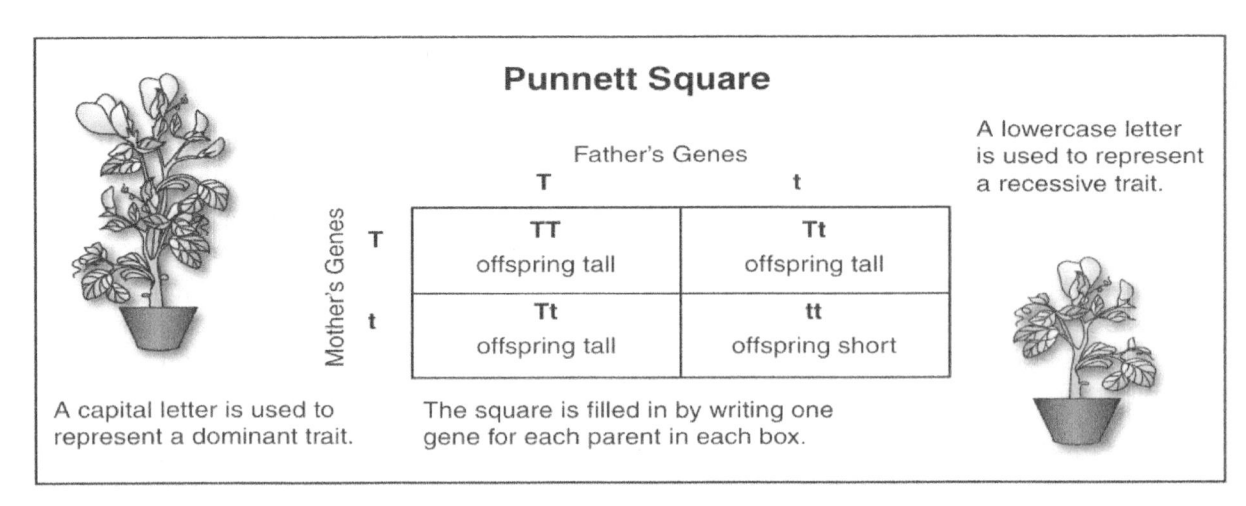

Father's Genes

	T	t
T	TT offspring tall	Tt offspring tall
t	Tt offspring tall	tt offspring short

Mother's Genes

A capital letter is used to represent a dominant trait.

A lowercase letter is used to represent a recessive trait.

The square is filled in by writing one gene for each parent in each box.

Look at the Punnett square for tallness in peas. The genetic makeup of an organism is its genotype. The **genotype** (genetic makeup) of the mother is **Tt**, and the genotype of the father is **Tt**. They each have a tall gene and a short gene, but because the tall gene is dominant, both plants appear tall. There are three possible genotypes for the offspring: **TT, Tt**, and **tt**. Using the Punnett square, scientists can predict that 75 percent, or #f, of the offspring will be tall plants. only a plant that inherits two short genes (**tt**) will be short.

Example question:

In a group of small dogs, some individuals have short fur and others have long fur. In this group, the gene for the fur length trait has two alleles. The allele for short fur (*F*) is dominant over the allele for long fur (*f*).

Complete the Punnett square below to show all possible genotypes of the offspring from a cross between two cats.

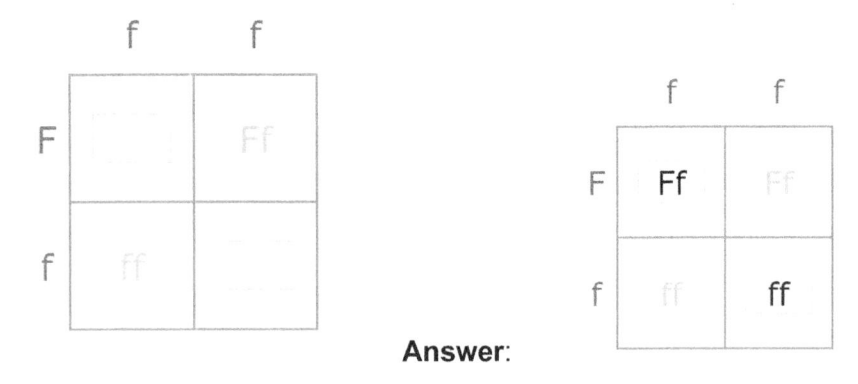

	f	f
F		Ff
f	ff	

	f	f
F	Ff	Ff
f	ff	ff

Answer:

By completing and interpreting Punnett squares, you can predict the possible genotypic and phenotypic outcomes of a genetic cross and understand the inheritance patterns of specific traits.

Chapter 5: Earth and Space Sciences

Earth science encompasses a wide range of topics, including geology, meteorology, oceanography, and environmental science. Through exploration and inquiry, students will gain a deeper understanding of the Earth's processes and systems.

- Earth's systems: Geosphere, hydrosphere, atmosphere, and biosphere
- Earth processes: Weathering, erosion, and plate tectonics
- Space systems: The solar system and beyond

Key concepts of Earth Science:

Solar System	The sun is the center of our solar system. It is the largest body in our solar system. Nine planets follow paths called orbits around the sun. The shape of each orbit is called an ellipse. An ellipse is a flattened circle
Earth's Structure	The Earth is composed of several layers, including the solid inner core, liquid outer core, mantle, and crust. Students will learn about the composition, properties, and interactions of these layers, as well as the processes that shape the Earth's surface, such as plate tectonics, erosion, and weathering.
Rocks and Minerals:	Rocks and minerals are the building blocks of the Earth's crust. Students will explore the properties and classification of minerals, as well as the formation and identification of different types of rocks, including igneous, sedimentary, and metamorphic rocks.
Earth's Atmosphere:	The Earth's atmosphere is a dynamic layer of gases that surrounds the planet. Students will investigate the composition and structure of the atmosphere, atmospheric phenomena such as weather and climate, and the factors that influence weather patterns, including temperature, humidity, air pressure, and wind.
Water Cycle	The water cycle is the continuous movement of water between the Earth's surface and the atmosphere. Students will learn about the processes of evaporation, condensation, precipitation, and runoff, as well as the role of oceans in regulating the Earth's climate, storing carbon dioxide, and supporting marine life.
Natural and man-made resources and Greenhouse effect	Students will learn about the Renewable and non- Renewable resources and Green house effect details.

Let's explore each topic:

Solar System

In this section, students will embark on an exciting exploration of the solar system, the vast expanse of space that includes the Sun, planets, moons, asteroids, comets, and other celestial bodies.

The sun is the center of our solar system. It is the largest body in our solar system. Nine planets follow paths called orbits around the sun. The shape of each orbit is called an **ellipse**. An ellipse is a flattened circle

Earth

- Description: The third planet from the Sun, Earth is the only known planet to support life.
- Characteristics: It has a diverse range of ecosystems, including land, oceans, and atmosphere. and oxygen, and liquid water, which is essential for life.
- Features: Earth has a solid surface, an atmosphere composed mainly of nitrogen
- Significance: Earth's unique conditions make it a habitable planet, hosting a vast array of life forms, including humans.

Sun

- Description: The Sun is a star located at the center of the solar system, providing light, heat, and energy to the planets.
- Characteristics: It is a nearly perfect sphere of hot plasma, primarily composed of hydrogen and helium. helium and releasing immense amounts of energy.
- Features: The Sun's core undergoes nuclear fusion, converting hydrogen into
- Significance: The Sun's energy drives weather patterns, ocean currents, and photosynthesis on Earth, making it essential for sustaining life.

Moon

- Description: Earth's natural satellite, the Moon orbits around our planet.
- Characteristics: It has a rocky surface with impact craters, mountains, and maria (large, dark plains). experiences extreme temperature variations.
- Features: The Moon has no atmosphere or liquid water, and its surface
- Significance: The Moon's gravitational pull causes tides on Earth and has influenced cultural, religious, and scientific endeavors throughout human history.

Planets

Inner Planets (Terrestrial Planets): Mercury, Venus, Earth, Mars.

- Characteristics: Rocky surfaces, relatively small sizes, and thin or nonexistent atmospheres.
- Features: Mercury is closest to the Sun, Venus has a thick atmosphere with a runaway greenhouse effect, and Mars has polar ice caps and evidence of past water.

Outer Planets (Gas Giants): Jupiter, Saturn, Uranus, Neptune.

- Characteristics: Large sizes, primarily composed of hydrogen and helium, and thick atmospheres.
- Features: Jupiter is the largest planet with a prominent Great Red Spot, Saturn has a ring system, Uranus and Neptune have icy compositions and unique rotational axes.

Dwarf Planets: Pluto, Eris, Haumea, Makemake, Ceres.

- Characteristics: Smaller than the eight major planets, categorized as dwarf planets by the International Astronomical Union (IAU).
- Features: Pluto, once considered the ninth planet, has a complex system of moons and a tenuous atmosphere.

Brief description of the properties of some of the planets in our solar system:

1. Mercury: • Mercury is the smallest planet in our solar system and the closest to the sun. • It has no atmosphere to speak of, and its surface experiences extreme temperature variations, with scorching temperatures during the day and freezing temperatures at night.

2. Venus: • Venus is often called Earth's "sister planet" because of its similar size and composition. • It has a thick atmosphere composed mainly of carbon dioxide, which creates a runaway greenhouse effect, making Venus the hottest planet in our solar system, even hotter than Mercury.

3. Earth: • Earth is the only planet known to support life. • It has a diverse range of ecosystems, abundant liquid water on its surface, and a breathable atmosphere primarily composed of nitrogen and oxygen.

4. Mars: • Mars is often called the "Red Planet" because of its reddish appearance due to iron oxide (rust) on its surface. • It has a thin atmosphere composed mostly of carbon dioxide and its surface features include large volcanoes, valleys, and polar ice caps.

5. Jupiter: • Jupiter is the largest planet in our solar system and is known for its massive size and distinctive banded appearance caused by its swirling cloud patterns. • It has a strong magnetic field and numerous moons, including the four largest known as the Galilean moons: Io, Europa, Ganymede, and Callisto.

6. Saturn: • Saturn is famous for its spectacular ring system, composed of icy particles and rocky debris. • It is the second-largest planet in our solar system and has a relatively low density, which means it could theoretically float in water.

7. Uranus: • Uranus is an ice giant planet with a bluish-green hue due to the presence of methane in its atmosphere. • It has a unique rotational axis that is tilted almost 90 degrees relative to its orbit around the sun, causing it to appear to roll on its side as it orbits.

8. Neptune: • Neptune is the farthest planet from the sun and is similar in composition • It has a dynamic atmosphere with high-speed winds and the fastest known winds in the solar system.

Phases of Moon:

The phases of the moon refer to the different appearances of the moon as it orbits around the Earth. Here's an overview of the main phases:

- New Moon: The moon is not visible from Earth because it is positioned between the Earth and the Sun, with its illuminated side facing away from us.
- Waxing Crescent: A small sliver of the moon becomes visible on the right side (in the Northern Hemisphere) of the moon's disk, gradually increasing in size each night.
- First Quarter: Half of the moon's disk is illuminated, creating a right-angle shape when viewed from Earth. This is often referred to as the "half moon."
- Waxing Gibbous: More than half of the moon's disk is illuminated, but it is not yet a full moon. The illuminated portion continues to grow larger each night.
- Full Moon: The entire disk of the moon is illuminated, appearing as a complete circle or disk in the night sky.
- Waning Gibbous: Following the full moon, the illuminated portion of the moon begins to decrease, but it is still more than half illuminated.
- Last Quarter: Half of the moon's disk is illuminated, but this time, it is the left side that is illuminated. This phase is also referred to as the "half moon," but it is the opposite side illuminated compared to the first quarter.
- Waning Crescent: A small sliver of the moon becomes visible on the left side (in the Northern Hemisphere) of the moon's disk, gradually decreasing in size each night until it becomes a new moon again.

These phases repeat in a predictable cycle, known as the lunar cycle, which takes approximately 29.5 days to complete.

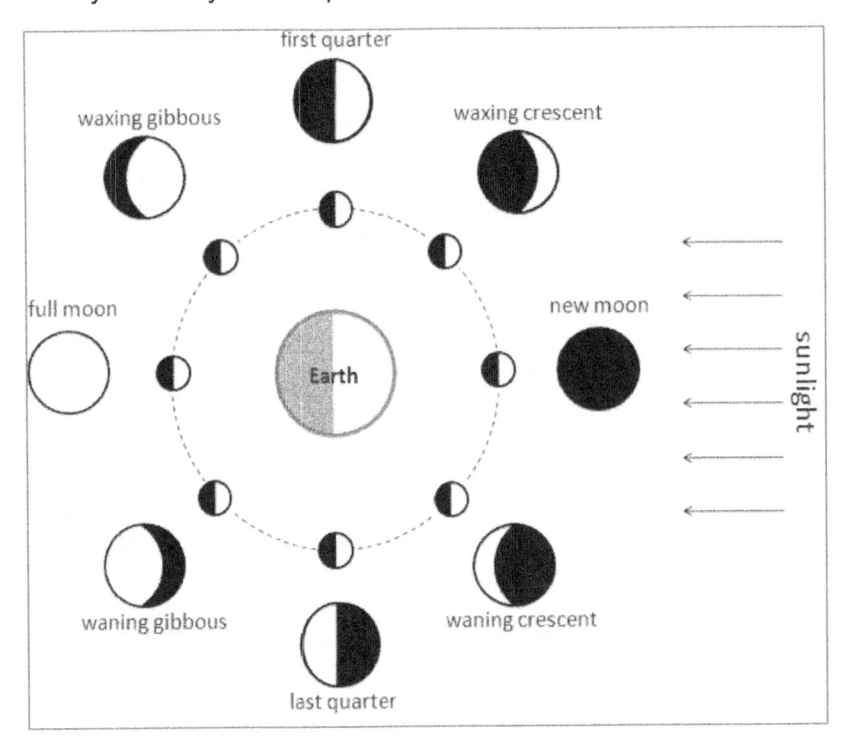

Eclipses—solar and lunar

Solar and lunar eclipses are fascinating astronomical events that occur when the Earth, moon, and sun align in specific ways.

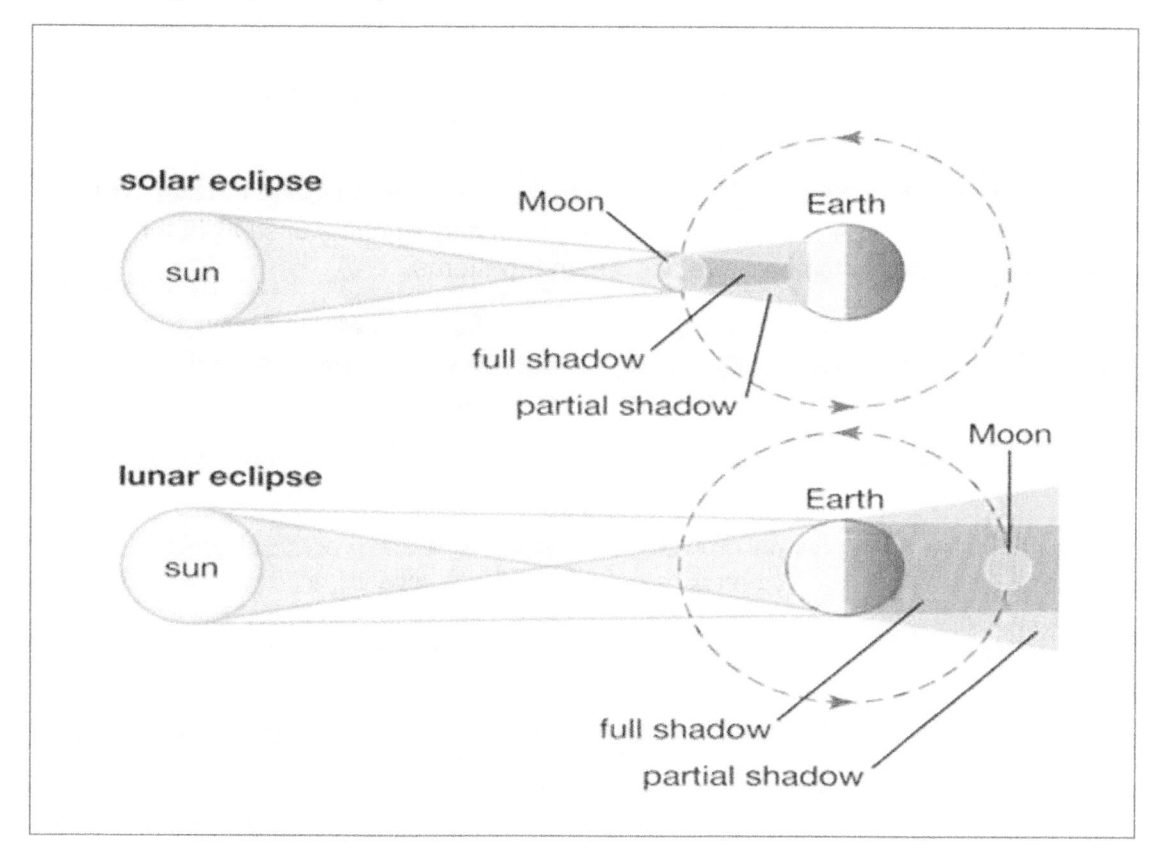

Solar Eclipse:

A solar eclipse occurs when the moon passes between the Earth and the sun, blocking all or part of the sun's light from reaching the Earth.

There are three types of solar eclipses: total, partial, and annular. In a total solar eclipse, the moon completely covers the sun, casting a shadow on Earth and creating a temporary darkness in the areas under the path of totality. During a partial solar eclipse, only a portion of the sun is obscured by the moon. An annular solar eclipse happens when the moon is too far from Earth to completely cover the sun, resulting in a ring of sunlight around the moon's edges.

Solar eclipses are relatively rare events and can only be observed from specific locations on Earth where the alignment of the sun, moon, and Earth is just right.

Lunar Eclipse:

• A lunar eclipse occurs when the Earth passes between the sun and the moon, causing the Earth's shadow to fall on the moon.

• Like solar eclipses, there are three types of lunar eclipses: total, partial, and penumbral. In a total lunar eclipse, the Earth's shadow completely covers the moon, giving it a reddish-brown hue known as a "blood moon." During a partial lunar eclipse, only a portion of the moon passes through the Earth's shadow. A penumbral lunar eclipse occurs when the moon passes through the faint outer part of the Earth's shadow, causing a subtle darkening of the lunar surface.

• Lunar eclipses are more common than solar eclipses and can be observed from any location on Earth where the moon is above the horizon during the eclipse.

Seasons, revolution and rotation on earth

• Seasons are the result of the tilt of the Earth's axis relative to its orbit around the sun. As the Earth orbits the sun, different parts of the planet receive varying amounts of sunlight throughout the year, leading to changes in temperature and weather patterns.

• There are four primary seasons: spring, summer, autumn (fall), and winter. These seasons occur because different hemispheres of the Earth receive more direct sunlight at different times of the year, depending on their tilt toward or away from the sun.

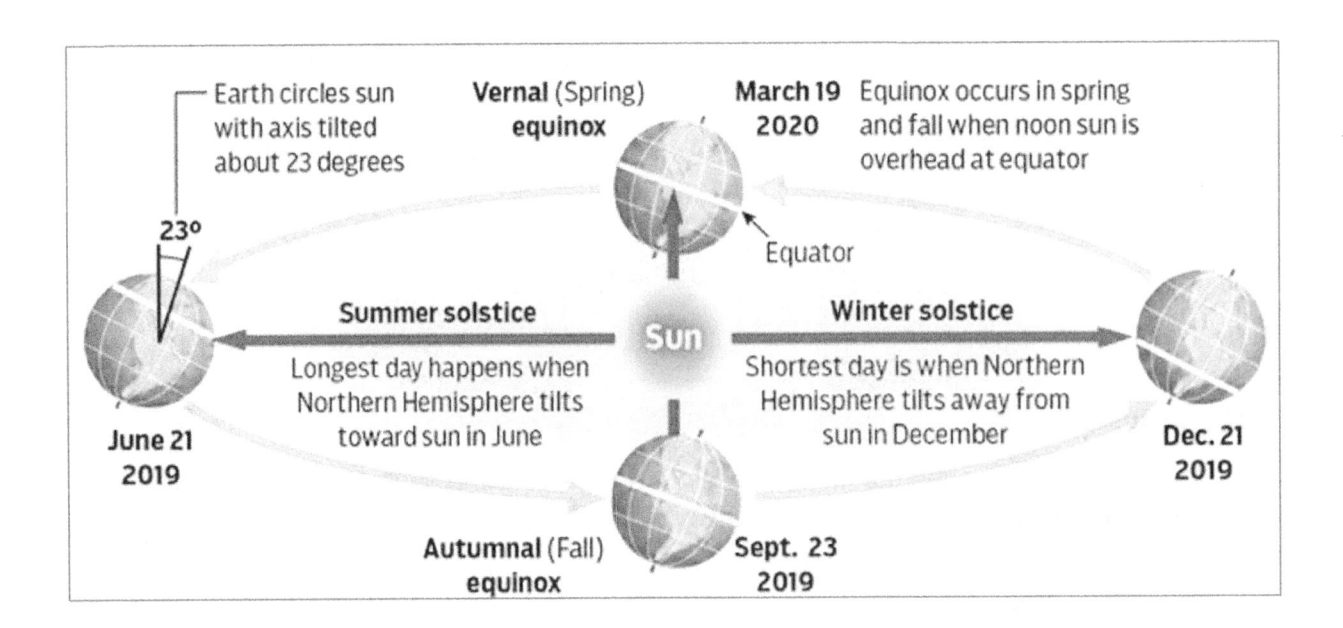

Revolution: Earth's revolution refers to its orbit around the sun. It takes approximately 365.25 days for the Earth to complete one orbit around the sun, which defines a year. This orbital path is not a perfect circle but an elliptical shape, with the sun located at one of the two foci of the ellipse. As the Earth revolves around the sun, it maintains a relatively constant tilt on its axis, which is approximately 23.5 degrees. This tilt is the primary reason for the **changing seasons.**

Rotation: Earth's rotation refers to its spinning on its axis, which is an imaginary line passing through the North and South Poles. The Earth completes one full rotation approximately every 24 hours, defining a day. The rotation of the Earth is responsible for the alternation between **day and night**. As the Earth rotates, different parts of its surface are exposed to sunlight or darkness, creating the cycle of day and night.

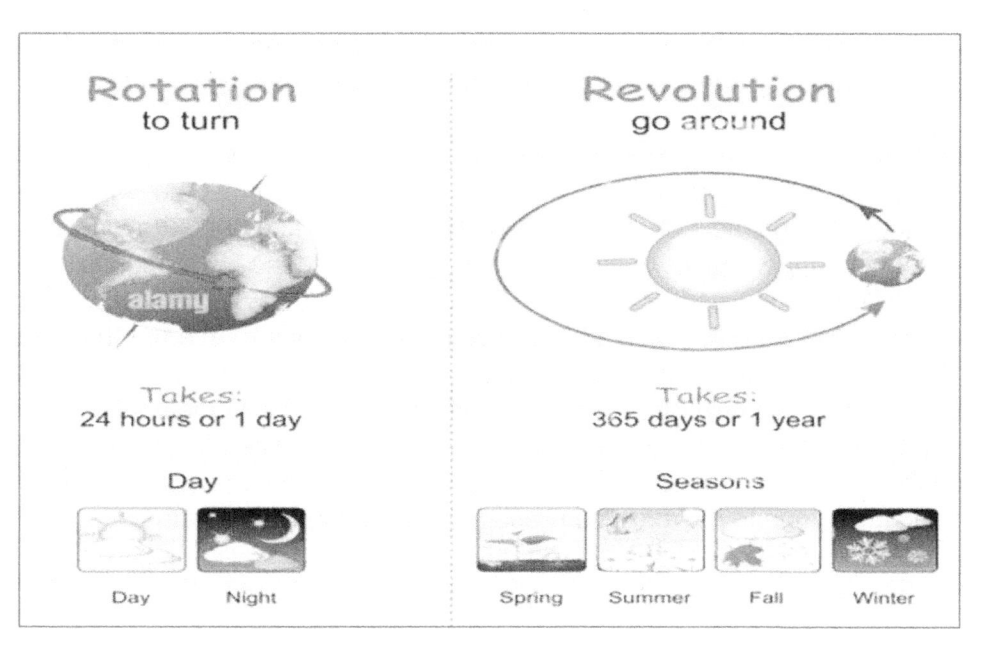

Rotation — to turn
Takes: 24 hours or 1 day
Day / Night

Revolution — go around
Takes: 365 days or 1 year
Seasons: Spring, Summer, Fall, Winter

Gravity in Our Solar System :

Eight planets orbit the Sun and are held in place due to gravity. Gravity is the attractive force by which a planet or other body draws objects toward its center. Anything that has mass also has gravity. The larger an object's mass, the larger its gravitational force is on another object. Since the mass of the Sun is so large compared to the planets, its force of gravity keeps all of the planets in orbit around it. Gravity also keeps other bodies in orbit, such as moons. Moons most often orbit a planet, but even a large space rock (asteroid) can hold a small moon in orbit due to the gravitational pull between the two objects. Gravity also holds the rock and ice that make up Saturn's rings in orbit.

Beyond the Solar System: Beyond the solar system lies a vast expanse of space filled with stars, galaxies, and other celestial objects.

Galaxies

Our solar system is one of many in the Milky Way galaxy. A galaxy is a huge collection of gas, dust, and billions of stars, and their solar systems are all held together by gravity. When you look up at stars in the night sky, you are seeing other stars in the Milky Way galaxy. Our solar system only has one star, the Sun!

There are many galaxies besides the Milky Way

Earth's Structure

The Earth is composed of several layers, each with distinct properties and compositions. Additionally, the outermost layer of the Earth is broken into several large and small pieces known as tectonic plates. Here's a brief description of the Earth's layers and tectonic plates:

1. Crust: • The crust is the outermost layer of the Earth and is composed mainly of solid rock. • It is divided into two types: continental crust, which forms the continents and is thicker but

less dense, and oceanic crust, which underlies the ocean basins and is thinner but denser. • The crust is the thinnest layer of the Earth, ranging from about 5 to 70 kilometers in thickness.
2. Mantle: • The mantle lies beneath the crust and extends to a depth of about 2,900 kilometers. • It is composed of solid but flowing rock material called magma, which can deform and flow over long time scales due to high temperature and pressure. • The mantle is subdivided into the upper mantle, which is relatively rigid, and the lower mantle, which is more ductile and flows more readily.
3. Outer Core:. • The outer core lies beneath the mantle and extends from a depth of about 2,900 to 5,150 kilometers • It is composed primarily of molten iron and nickel, and it generates Earth's magnetic field through the movement of conductive materials.
4. Inner Core:. • The inner core is the innermost layer of the Earth, extending from a depth of about 5,150 kilometers to the center of the Earth at about 6,371 kilometers • It is composed of solid iron and nickel due to the extreme pressure despite high temperatures.

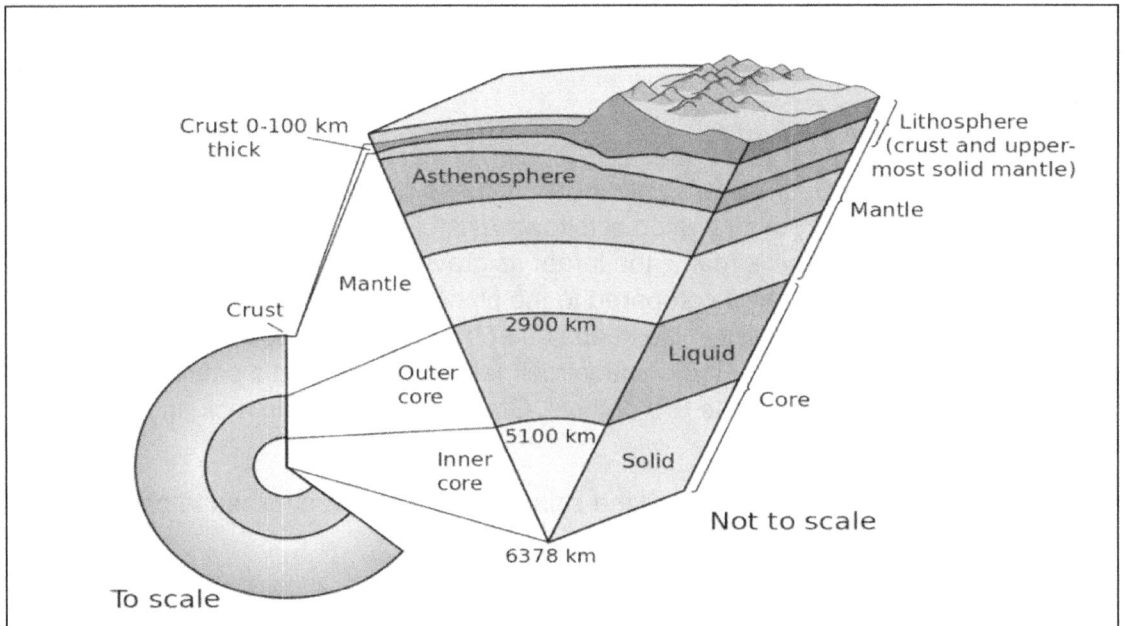

Tectonic Plates:

• The Earth's lithosphere, which includes the crust and the uppermost part of the mantle, is divided into several large and small pieces called tectonic plates.
• These plates float on the semi-fluid asthenosphere beneath them and move relative to each other due to the heat-driven convection currents in the mantle.
• The interactions between tectonic plates at their boundaries give rise to various geological phenomena, including earthquakes, volcanic activity, mountain formation, and the formation and closure of ocean basins.
• There are three main types of plate boundaries: **divergent boundaries** (where plates move apart), **convergent boundaries** (where plates move together), and **transform boundaries** (where plates slide past each other).

Plate Tectonics

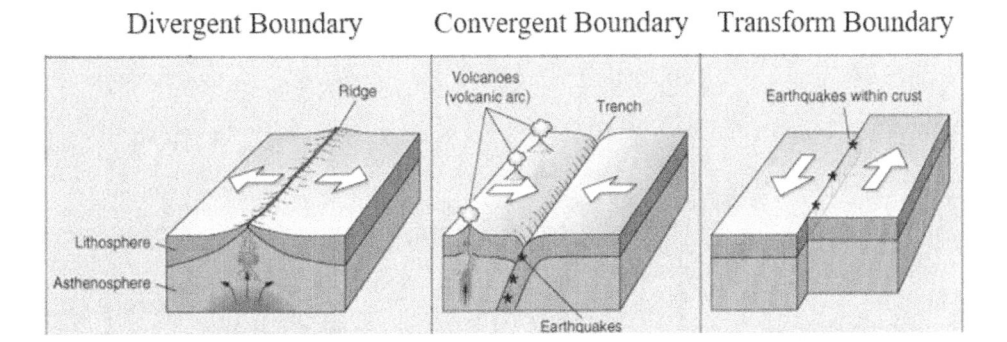

Divergent Boundary   **Convergent Boundary**   **Transform Boundary**

Rocks And Minerals

Rocks are solid, naturally occurring substances composed of minerals or mineral-like substances.

Rock Cycle:

The rock cycle describes the continuous processes by which rocks are formed, altered, destroyed, and re-formed over geological time. It involves various processes such as weathering and erosion, deposition, lithification, metamorphism, melting, and solidification. Rocks can undergo multiple transformations through the rock cycle. For example, igneous rocks can be weathered and eroded to form sediment, which can then become sedimentary rock. This sedimentary rock can undergo metamorphism to become metamorphic rock, which may subsequently melt to form magma and restart the cycle.

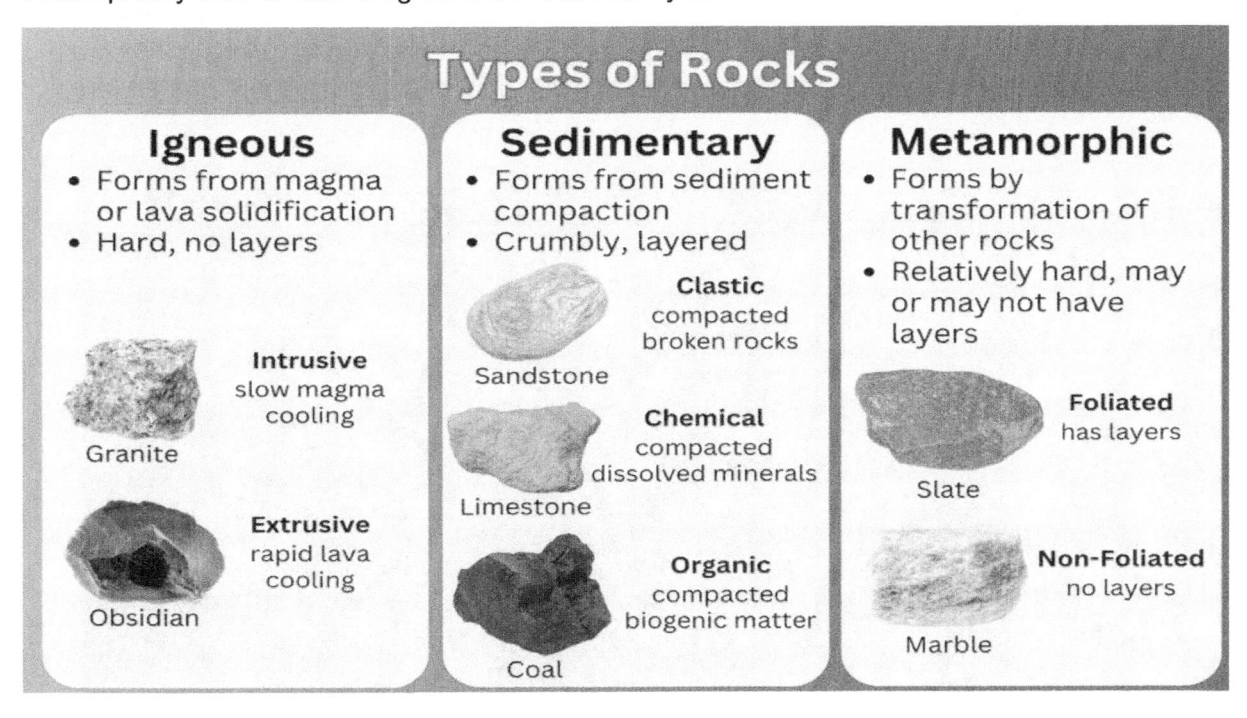

Types of Rocks

Igneous
- Forms from magma or lava solidification
- Hard, no layers

Granite — **Intrusive** slow magma cooling

Obsidian — **Extrusive** rapid lava cooling

Sedimentary
- Forms from sediment compaction
- Crumbly, layered

Sandstone — **Clastic** compacted broken rocks

Limestone — **Chemical** compacted dissolved minerals

Coal — **Organic** compacted biogenic matter

Metamorphic
- Forms by transformation of other rocks
- Relatively hard, may or may not have layers

Slate — **Foliated** has layers

Marble — **Non-Foliated** no layers

Rock Cycle

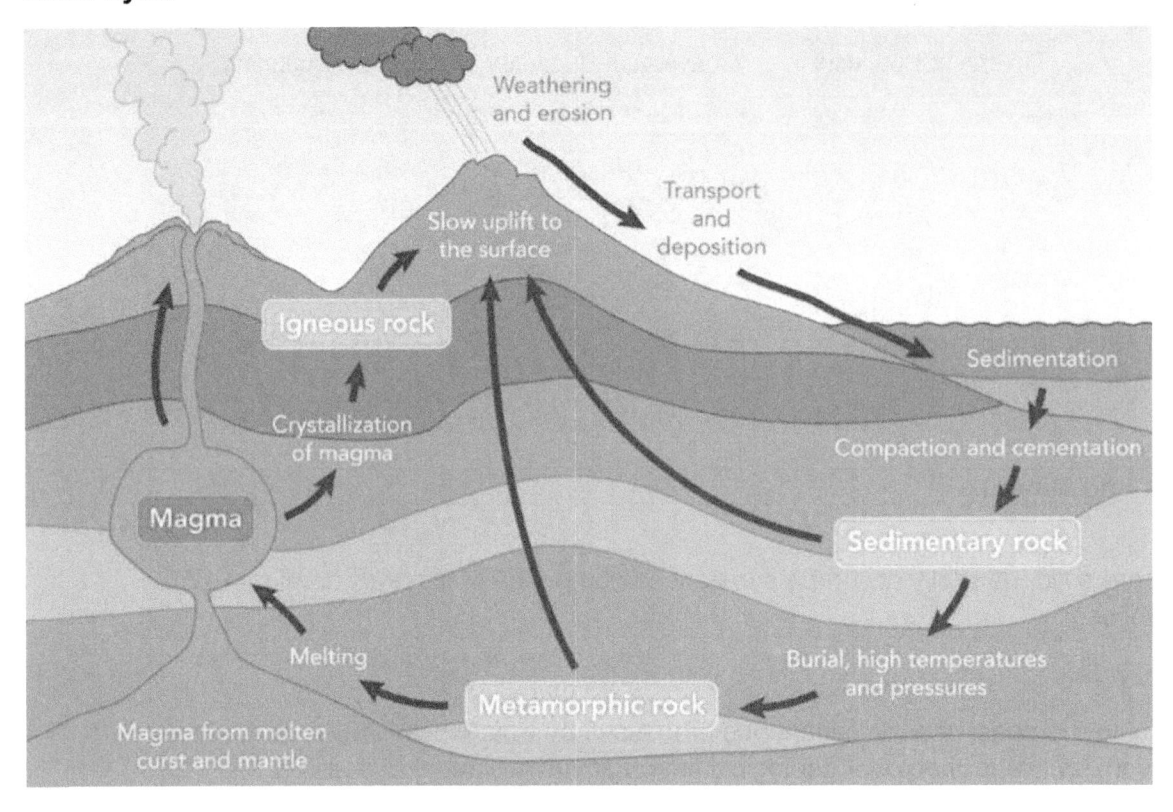

Mohs scale

The Mohs scale of mineral hardness is a qualitative ordinal scale that characterizes the scratch resistance of different minerals through the ability of a harder material to scratch a softer material. It was created by the German geologist and mineralogist Friedrich Mohs in 1812 and is one of several material science definitions of hardness, some of which are more quantitative.

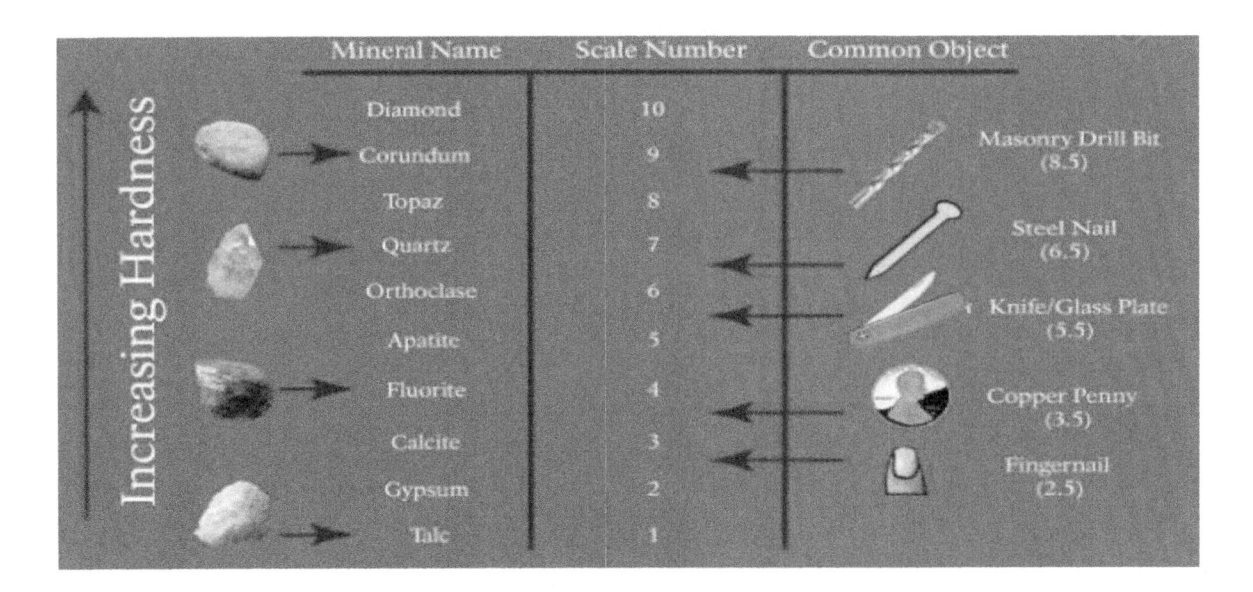

Mineral Name	Scale Number	Common Object
Diamond	10	
Corundum	9	Masonry Drill Bit (8.5)
Topaz	8	
Quartz	7	Steel Nail (6.5)
Orthoclase	6	Knife/Glass Plate (5.5)
Apatite	5	
Fluorite	4	Copper Penny (3.5)
Calcite	3	
Gypsum	2	Fingernail (2.5)
Talc	1	

Earth's Atmosphere

The atmosphere is comprised of layers based on temperature. These layers are the troposphere, stratosphere, mesosphere and thermosphere. A further region at about 500 km above the Earth's surface is called the exosphere.

More details are shown in figure below:

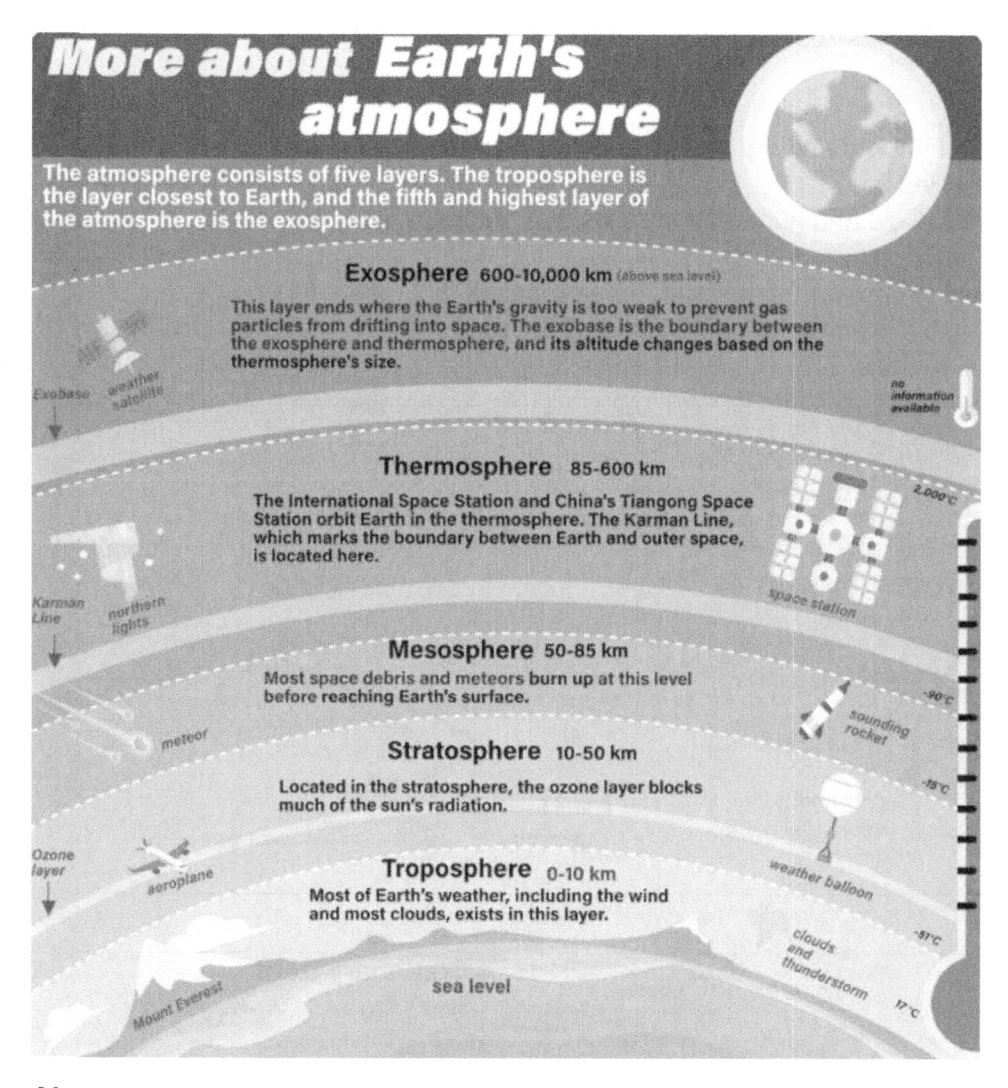

More about Earth's atmosphere

The atmosphere consists of five layers. The troposphere is the layer closest to Earth, and the fifth and highest layer of the atmosphere is the exosphere.

Exosphere 600-10,000 km (above sea level)
This layer ends where the Earth's gravity is too weak to prevent gas particles from drifting into space. The exobase is the boundary between the exosphere and thermosphere, and its altitude changes based on the thermosphere's size.
no information available

Thermosphere 85-600 km
The International Space Station and China's Tiangong Space Station orbit Earth in the thermosphere. The Karman Line, which marks the boundary between Earth and outer space, is located here.
2,000 °C

Mesosphere 50-85 km
Most space debris and meteors burn up at this level before reaching Earth's surface.
-90 °C

Stratosphere 10-50 km
Located in the stratosphere, the ozone layer blocks much of the sun's radiation.
-15 °C

Troposphere 0-10 km
Most of Earth's weather, including the wind and most clouds, exists in this layer.
-51 °C / 17 °C

sea level

Air masses

Air masses are large bodies of air that have relatively uniform temperature, humidity, and stability characteristics throughout their horizontal extent. They form over regions with consistent surface characteristics, such as ocean surfaces or large landmasses, and can cover thousands of square kilometers. Here's a brief description of air masses:

Classification: Air masses are classified based on their temperature and humidity characteristics and the regions where they originate. The two primary classifications are:

- Tropical: These air masses form in the low latitudes, near the equator, and are generally warm to hot and humid.
- Polar: These air masses form in high latitudes, near the poles, and are generally cold and dry.

Additional Classifications: • In addition to the primary classifications, air masses can be further classified based on their source regions:

• Continental: These air masses form over land surfaces and tend to be dry.

• Maritime: These air masses form over ocean surfaces and tend to be humid.

Types of Air Masses:

1. Continental Polar (cP): Cold and dry air masses that originate over polar regions. ocean surfaces near the poles.
2. Maritime Polar (mP): Cold and humid air masses that originate over over continental tropical regions.
3. Continental Tropical (cT): Warm to hot and dry air masses that originate
4. Maritime Tropical (mT): Warm to hot and humid air masses that originate over ocean surfaces in tropical regions.

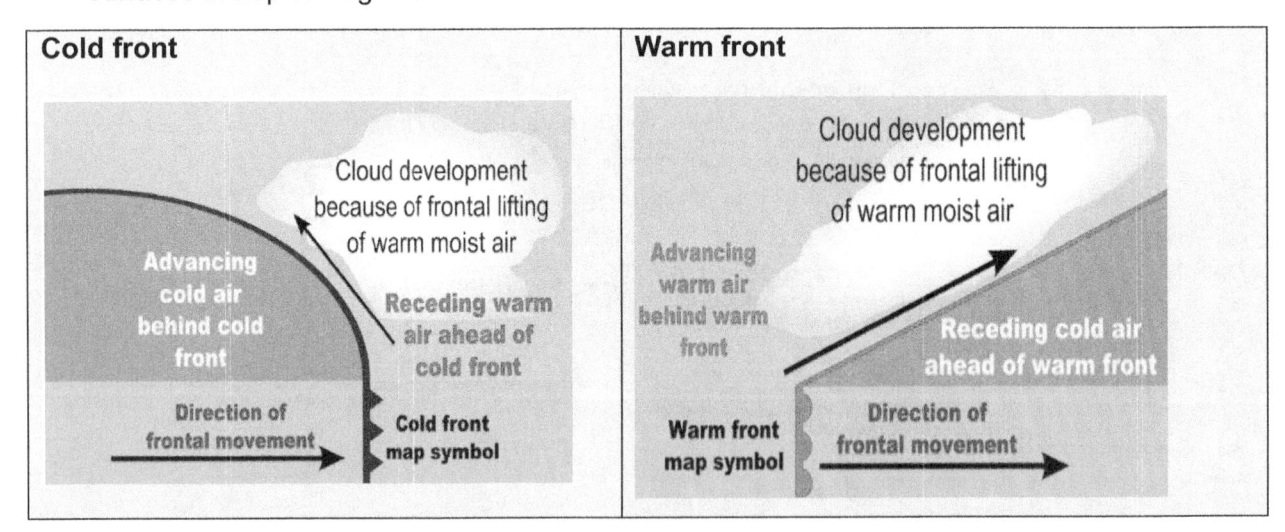

Cold front	Warm front
Cloud development because of frontal lifting of warm moist air. Advancing cold air behind cold front. Receding warm air ahead of cold front. Direction of frontal movement. Cold front map symbol.	Cloud development because of frontal lifting of warm moist air. Advancing warm air behind warm front. Receding cold air ahead of warm front. Warm front map symbol. Direction of frontal movement.

Occluded front	Stationary front

Latitude and longitude

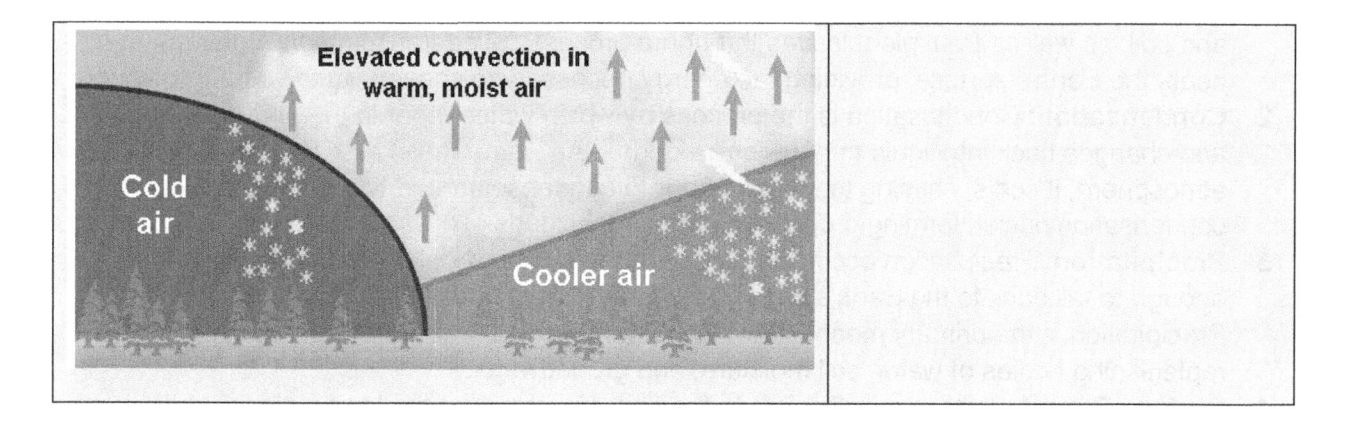

Latitude and longitude are geographic coordinates used to specify locations on the Earth's surface.

Latitude: Latitude lines, also known as parallels, run horizontally around the Earth and measure distances north or south of the equator, which is located at 0 degrees latitude. Latitude is expressed in degrees, with values ranging from 0 degrees at the equator to 90 degrees at the North and South Poles. Positive values indicate locations north of the equator, while negative values indicate locations south of the equator. Latitude lines are parallel to each other and do not intersect. They circle the Earth from east to west.

Longitude: Longitude lines, also known as meridians, run vertically from pole to pole and measure distances east or west of the prime meridian, which is located at 0 degrees longitude.

Longitude is also expressed in degrees, with values ranging from 0 degrees at the prime meridian to 180 degrees eastward and 180 degrees westward. Positive values indicate locations east of the prime meridian, while negative values indicate locations west of the prime meridian. Unlike latitude lines, longitude lines converge at the poles and are farthest apart at the equator.

Water Cycle

Water cycle

The water cycle, also known as the hydrological cycle, describes the continuous movement of water on, above, and below the surface of the Earth. It involves a series of processes by which water is evaporated from the Earth's surface, transported through the atmosphere, condensed into clouds, and returned to the Earth as precipitation.

Here's a brief description of the water cycle:

1. **Evaporation:** Evaporation is the process by which water is converted from liquid to vapor and enters the atmosphere. It occurs primarily from the surfaces of oceans, lakes, rivers,

and soil, as well as from plant leaves through a process called transpiration. Solar energy heats the Earth's surface, providing the energy necessary to convert liquid water into vapor.

2. **Condensation:** Condensation is the process by which water vapor in the atmosphere cools and changes back into liquid form to form clouds. • As warm, moist air rises in the atmosphere, it cools, causing the water vapor to condense around tiny particles called condensation nuclei, forming droplets that make up clouds.
3. **Precipitation**: Precipitation occurs when condensed water droplets in clouds grow large enough to fall back to the Earth's surface in the form of rain, snow, sleet, or hail. Precipitation is the primary means by which water returns to the Earth's surface, replenishing bodies of water, soil moisture, and groundwater.
4. **Surface Runoff**: Surface runoff refers to the flow of water over the land surface into streams, rivers, lakes, and oceans. It occurs when precipitation exceeds the infiltration capacity of the soil or when the ground is saturated with water. Surface runoff plays a crucial role in shaping the landscape and transporting sediment and nutrients.
5. **Infiltration and Groundwater Recharge**: Infiltration is the process by which precipitation soaks into the ground and replenishes soil moisture and groundwater. Some of the water that infiltrates the ground percolates downward through the soil and rock layers, eventually recharging groundwater reservoirs.
6. **Transpiration**: Transpiration is the release of water vapor from plants into the atmosphere through tiny openings in their leaves called stomata. It is an important component of the water cycle as it contributes to the moisture content of the atmosphere and influences local and regional climate patterns.

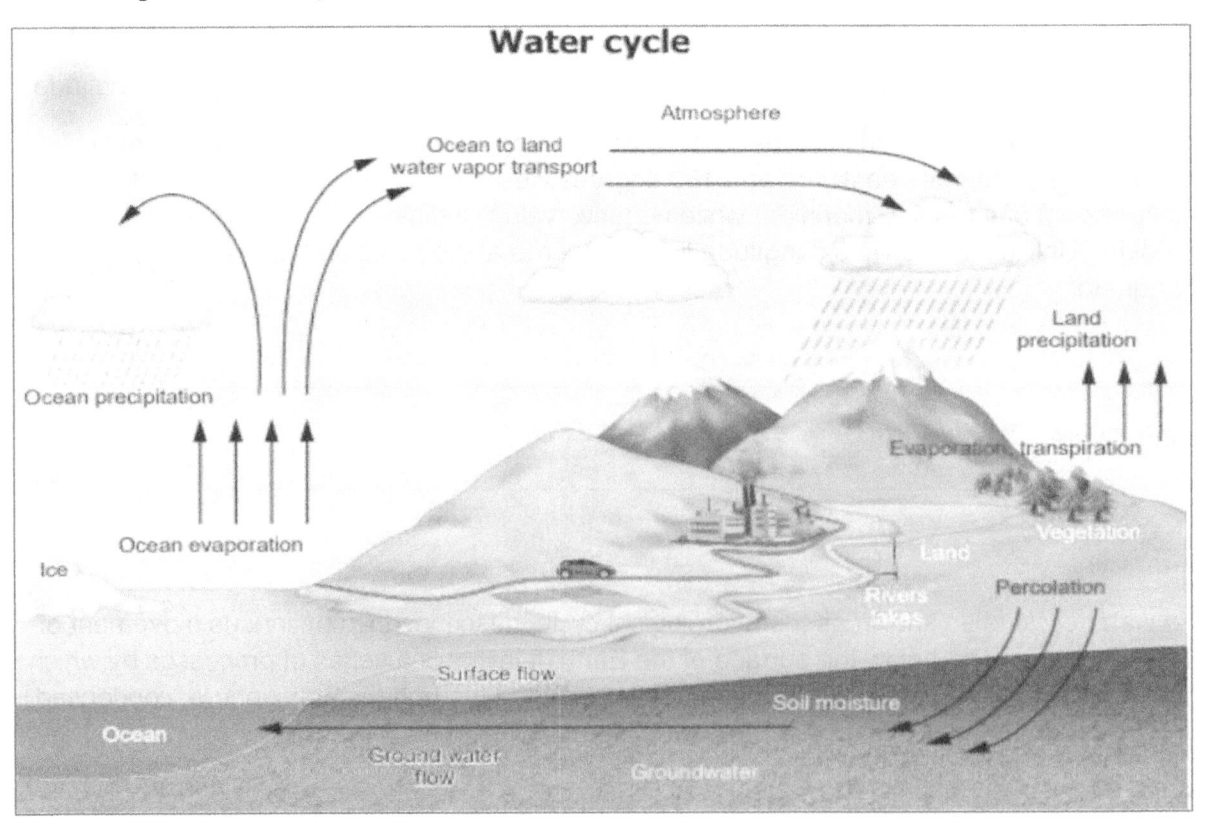

Natural and man-made resources, renewable and non-renewable

Renewable Resources:

Renewable resources are replenished naturally and can be sustained indefinitely with careful management. Examples include:

- Solar Energy: Energy from the sun, captured using solar panels for electricity generation or solar thermal systems for heating.
- Wind Energy: Energy harnessed from the wind using wind turbines to generate electricity. or dams, to generate electricity.
- Hydropower: Energy derived from flowing water, typically in rivers
- Biomass: Organic material derived from plants or animals, used for energy production or as raw materials for various products.
- Geothermal Energy: Heat energy from the Earth's interior, used for heating buildings or generating electricity.

Non-renewable Resources:

Non-renewable resources are finite and cannot be replaced within a human lifespan or at a rate comparable to their consumption. Examples include:

- Fossil Fuels: Such as coal, oil, and natural gas, formed from the remains of ancient plants and animals over millions of years.
- Minerals: Such as iron, copper, gold, and rare earth elements, extracted from the Earth's crust for various industrial purposes.
- Nuclear Energy: Derived from the fission of uranium or plutonium atoms, used for electricity generation in nuclear power plants.

Man-made Resources:

Synthetic Materials: Synthetic materials are created through chemical synthesis or manufacturing processes. • Examples include:

- Plastics: Synthetic polymers derived from petrochemicals, widely used in packaging, construction, and consumer goods.
- Composite Materials: Engineered materials made from a combination of two or more substances, such as fiberglass or carbon fiber composites.

Technological Innovations: Technological advancements and inventions that improve efficiency, productivity, and quality of life .Examples include.:

- Information Technology: Software, hardware, and digital services used for communication, data processing, and entertainment.
- Biotechnology: Genetic engineering, pharmaceuticals, and medical devices developed for healthcare and agriculture.

Green house effect

The greenhouse effect is a natural process that warms the Earth's surface. It occurs when certain gases in the Earth's atmosphere trap heat from the sun, preventing it from escaping back into space. While this process is essential for maintaining a habitable climate on Earth, human activities have intensified the greenhouse effect, leading to global warming and climate change.

Enhanced Greenhouse Effect:. • Human activities, such as burning fossil fuels (coal, oil, and natural gas), deforestation, and industrial processes, have significantly increased the concentration of greenhouse gases in the atmosphere • The increased levels of greenhouse gases intensify the natural greenhouse effect, leading to additional warming of the Earth's surface and lower atmosphere. • This phenomenon, known as the enhanced greenhouse effect or global warming, contributes to climate change, causing rising temperatures, melting glaciers and ice caps, sea level rise, changes in precipitation patterns, and more frequent and intense extreme weather events.

Impacts of Climate Change:. • Climate change resulting from the enhanced greenhouse effect has far reaching impacts on ecosystems, human societies, and economies • These impacts include disruptions to agriculture and food security, loss of biodiversity, increased frequency of heatwaves, droughts, floods, and storms, displacement of populations due to sea-level rise, and threats to infrastructure and coastal communities.

Efforts to mitigate the greenhouse effect and address climate change include reducing greenhouse gas emissions through policies, regulations, and technological innovations, transitioning to renewable energy sources, promoting energy efficiency and conservation measures, and implementing adaptation strategies to cope with the impacts of climate change.

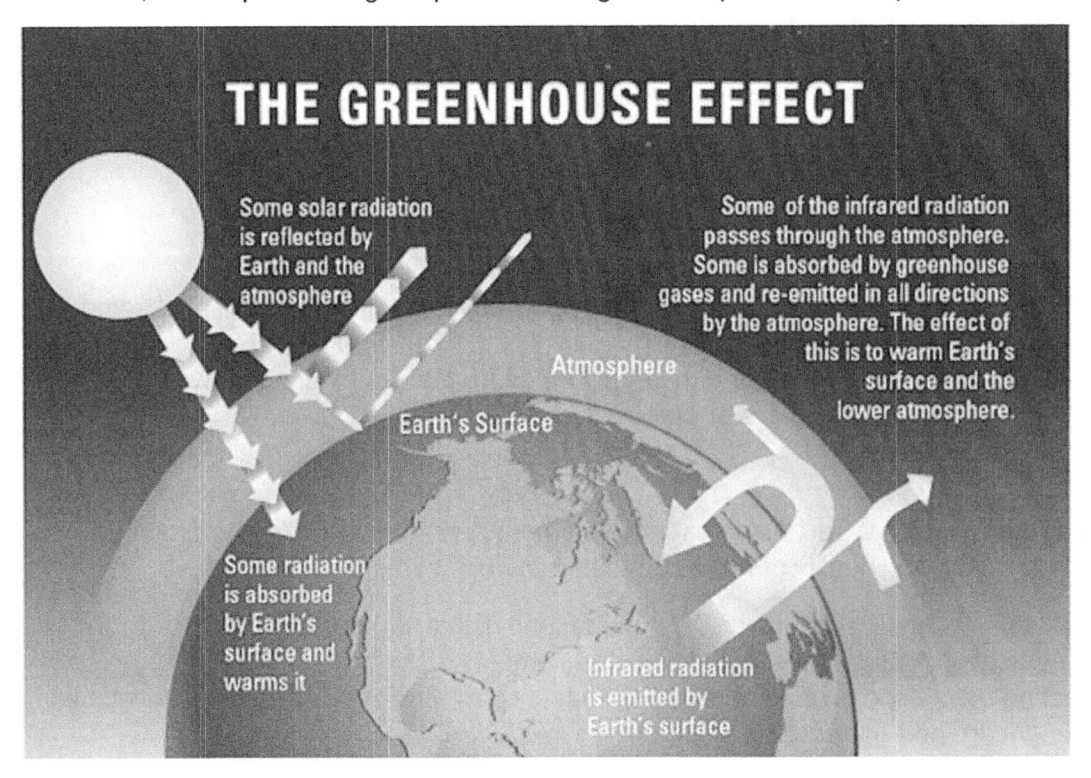

Practice Worksheets

In the following section, you'll find practice worksheets, each consisting of 15 questions.

It's essential to time yourself during these tests, each test designed to be completed within a 10 to 12 minutes timeframe.

Worksheet 1

Date	Start time	End Time	Score

1. The new moon is followed by which major lunar phase?

(A) Waning crescent	(B) Waxing crescent
(C) Waning gibbous	(D) Waxing gibbous

2. Individuals with favorable traits survive, reproduce and pass on their traits to their offspring. What is this process called?

(A) Mutation	(B) Evolution
(C) Adaptation	(D) Natural selection

3. Which of these is an incorrect statement about Neptune?

(A) Neptune is the coldest planet	(B) Neptune has rings around it
(C) Neptune is the slowest revolving planet	(D) None of these

4. Select the Law of Motion most relevant to the following situation: While roller blading, Tom exerted force against the ground, subsequently propelling himself forward. Choose all that are applicable.

(A) 1st Law of Motion	(B) 2nd Law of Motion
(C) 3rd Law of Motion	(D) None

5. The resistance experienced by an object while it moves across another surface is termed as

(A) Unbalanced	(B) Inertia
(C) Friction	(D) Acceleration

6. Which of the following presents a safety hazard while working in the science laboratory?

(A) knowing how to use equipment	(B) wearing safety goggles
(C) following directions	(D) working alone

7. Which of the following is a unit of energy?

(A) Newton	(B) Joule
(C) Watt	(D) Pascal

8. What type of energy is stored in a stretched rubber band?

(A) Kinetic energy	(B) Thermal energy
(C) Potential energy	(D) Chemical energy

9. Which of the following best describes an atom?

(A) protons and electrons grouped together in a random pattern	(B) protons and electrons grouped together in an alternating pattern
(C) a core of protons and neutrons surrounded by electrons	(D) a core of electrons and neutrons surrounded by protons

10. Students create a table that lists processes observed in nature. Which process describes only a physical change?

Process	Change
1	Fungus decomposing organic matter
2	Leaves using carbon dioxide to make sugar
3	Plants using nitrogen to make protein
4	Water evaporating from salt water

(A) Process 1	(B) Process 2
(C) Process 3	(D) Process 4

11. Which of the following best describes Newton's Third Law of Motion?

(A) An object in motion stays in motion.	(B) Force equals mass times acceleration.
(C) For every action, there is an equal and opposite reaction	(D) Energy cannot be created or destroyed.

12. Which two body systems are primarily responsible for locomotion?

(A) Skeletal system and muscular system	(B) Nervous system and circulatory system
(C) Respiratory system and digestive system	(D) Integumentary system and excretory system

13. Which statement about stars is correct?

(A) Star formation begins in a nebula.	(B) Star formation begins in a nebula.
(C) Supergiants are stars that can absorb black holes.	(D) Main-sequence stars are formed by comets.

14. Selective breeding can be used to produce

(A) Physical traits	(B) Behavioral traits
(C) Both A an B are true	(D) None of the option is true

15. Within a substance, atoms that collide frequently and move independently of one another are most likely in a

(A) liquid	(B) solid
(C) gas	(D) crystal

71

Worksheet 2

Date	Start time	End Time	Score

1. Which statement describes the energy changes that occur when water in a tea kettle is heated on a stove that uses natural gas?

(A) Some of the chemical energy in the natural gas transforms into thermal energy, which heats the water. Then some of the thermal energy changes into sound energy when the water forms steam and the steam leave the kettle.	(B) Some of the thermal energy in the natural gas transforms into sound energy when the water becomes hot. Then some of the sound energy changes into light energy when the kettle becomes warm.
(C) Some of the electrical energy in the natural gas transforms into thermal energy, which causes the water to form steam. Then some of the thermal energy changes into sound energy and light energy when the steam leaves the kettle.	(D) Some of the light energy in the natural gas transforms into chemical energy in the water. Then some of the chemical energy changes into kinetic energy when steam leaves the kettle and into sound energy when the water boils

2. Which of the following forms of energy is associated with the motion of objects?

(A) Chemical energy	(B) Nuclear energy
(C) Kinetic energy	(D) Gravitational potential energy

3. Which of the following is found farthest from the center of an atom?

(A) nucleus	(B) proton
(C) neutron	(D) electron

4. If a force of 10 N is applied to an object and moves it 5 meters in the direction of the force, what is the work done on the object?

(A) 2 Joules	(B) 15 Joules
(C) 50 Joules	(D) 100 Joules

5. Choose which Law of Motion is best described below: When John was rollerblading, he pushed against the ground and then he rolled forward. Choose all that apply.

(A) First Law of Motion	(B) Second Law of Motion
(C) Third Law of Motion	(D) none

6. Rilla wanted to see if the solid substance is an acid or a base. In which order she should do the following steps
    A. Test with blue litmus paper
    B. Dissolve the substance in water
    C. Look at any changes in the color of the litmus paper
    D. Grind some of the substance to make a powder.

(A) ADBC	(B) BACD
(C) CBAD	(D) DBAC

7. The resistance that one object has when moving over another object is known as

(A) Inertia	(B) Friction
(C) Acceleration	(D) Velocity

8. Which law is best applying if, Mia put her phone on the dashboard. She had to stop the car suddenly when a dog ran across the street. Mia's cell phone crashed into the windshield.

(A) First Law of Motion	(B) Second Law of Motion
(C) Third Law of Motion	(D) none

9. The diagram models four lunar phases. During which lunar phase is the tide highest?

(A) Phase 1	(B) Phase 2
(C) Phase 3	(D) Phase 4

10. A fitness trainer records the distance an athlete runs during three different trials.

Trial	Time (minutes)	Distance (kilometers)
1	15	4.5
2	30	9.0
3	45	13.5

What is the athlete's average speed in kilometers per minute?

(A) 0.3	(B) 0.5
(C) 4	(D) 2

11. Tim mixed two substances in four beakers, and placed a thermometer in each beaker. He checked the thermometers every minute for five minutes, and recorded the temperature in the table.

Time (minutes)	Beaker A (°C)	Beaker B (°C)	Beaker C (°C)	Beaker D (°C)
0	20	20	20	20
1	21	19	21	20
2	22	18	22	20
3	20	18	23	20
4	20	17	24	20
5	20	16	25	20

Which beaker shows the greatest temperature change over five minutes?

(A) Beaker A	(B) Beaker B
(C) Beaker C ✓	(D) Beaker D

12. GMOs stand for

(A) Genetic mutation Organism	(B) Genetically mutated operators
(C) Genetically modified organism ✓	(D) Germinating modified operators

13. What is the primary goal of gene therapy?

(A) To change an individual's physical appearance	(B) To cure diseases by replacing, inactivating, or introducing genes in cells ✓
(C) To increase an individual's athletic performance	(D) To alter a person's diet for better health

14. What do artificial selection and natural selection have in common?

(A) They are both methods for passing on traits ✓	(B) They both occur in the natural world
(C) They can both be used for gene therapy	(D) They both can both be controlled in a laboratory

15. Chris made the following table after collecting different kind of woods. The densities of four different woods are shown below. Which wood will sink when placed in a fluid with a density of 1.14?

Wood Sample Densities

Type of Wood	Density ($\frac{g}{cm^3}$)
African Teakwood	0.98
Balsa	0.14
Cedar	0.55
Ironwood	1.23

(A) African teakwood	(B) balsa
(C) cedar	(D) ironwood ✓

74

Worksheet 3

Date	Start time	End Time	Score

1. The diagram shows Earth in its orbit around the sun when very little light is visible at Earth's South Pole.

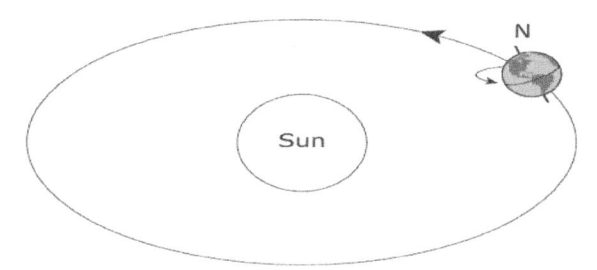

Which statement is true when Earth is in the position shown?

(A) It is August in the Northern Hemisphere. It is April in the Southern Hemisphere.	(B) It is summer in the Northern Hemisphere. It is winter in the Southern Hemisphere.
(C) The number of hours of daylight is greater in the Southern Hemisphere than in the Northern Hemisphere.	(D) Spring begins earlier in the year in the Southern Hemisphere than it does in the Northern Hemisphere.

2. A large redwood tree is measured to be about 100 units tall. Which unit is the most use?

(A) millimeters	(B) centimeters
(C) meters	(D) kilometers

3. If a ball is rolling down a hill

(A) The only force at work is gravity	(B) The only force at work is friction
(C) There are several forces working at the same time	(D) The laws of motion do not apply because gravity is pulling the boulder down the hill

4. A Kris pushes a 51.5-kilogram table across a smooth floor with a net force of 67 N. What is the approximate acceleration of the table?

(A) 1.3 m/s²	(B) 3450.5 m/s²
(C) 15.5 m/s²	(D) 0.77 m/s²

5. Which pair of elements are nonmetals and gases at room temperature and normal atmospheric pressure?

(A) Fluorine, F, and chlorine, Cl	(B) Boron, B, and aluminum, Al
(C) Hydrogen, H, and cesium, Cs	(D) Cobalt, Co, and nickel, Ni

75

6. What is speciation?

(A) Organisms that are similar but have different names, such as a tortoise and a turtle	(B) As a population develops new traits, it may eventually become a separate species with unique characteristics from the original organism
(C) Animals dying off because they are not the fittest for their environment	(D) The number of animals living in a space

7. The fine lead used in mechanical pencils has a diameter of about

(A) 0.5 centimeters	(B) 5.0 centimeters
(C) 0.5 millimeters	(D) 5.0 millimeters

8. When a big truck crashes into a wall and and both the truck and the wall are damaged, this is the result of which law of motion?

(A) First Law of Motion	(B) Second Law of Motion
(C) Third Law of Motion	(D) none

9. The following table shows properties of four different sample materials. One of these materials is cork, a type of wood that floats in water. Given that the density of water is 1 gm/ml, which of the samples is most likely cork?

Physical Properties

Sample Number	Mass	Volume
1	89 g	10 mL
2	26 g	10 mL
3	24 g	100 mL
4	160 g	100 mL

(A) 3	(B) 2
(C) 1	(D) 4

10. Mr. Jared digs a small pond in a pasture at his farmland. He adds young individuals from two species of algae-eating fish to the pond and plants some reeds around the edges of the pond. He wants the pond to be a sustainable ecosystem. Which of the following would be most helpful in increasing the pond ecosystem's sustainability?

(A) Decreasing the number of plant species around the edges of the pond	(B) Introducing older fish of the same species into the population of algae-eating fish
(C) Having a greater diversity of living organisms in the pond	(D) Adding gravel between the water and where the reeds are planted

11. For Every action there is

| (A) An equal but different reaction | (B) Two more forces |
| (C) An equal and opposite reaction | (D) A hidden force |

12. Which statement best describes cell theory?

| (A) Cells are part of complex organisms that work together to produce new cells. | (B) Cells perform a single life function, and most cells come from existing cells. |
| (C) Cells use energy from food to be able to perform life functions and work together to produce new cells. | (D) Cells are the basic unit of structure for all organisms, and all cells come from existing cells. |

13. Plants that live on the floors of densely populated forests must compete for sunlight. Which type of leaves are most likely found on plants that are best suited to living on the floor of a dense forest?

| (A) Leaves that are needle-shaped | (B) Leaves that are smallest |
| (C) Leaves that store the greatest amount of water | (D) Leaves with the greatest amount of surface area |

14. An object's tendency to stay in the same state until a force acts upon it is known as

| (A) Velocity | (B) Inertia |
| (C) Momentum | (D) Acceleration |

15. Cheetahs are the fastest land animal in the world. According to the theory of natural selection, how did the cheetah get to be so fast?

| (A) Cheetahs saw how fast rabbits were, so they started practicing running until they got to be really fast | (B) Cheetah cubs randomly had genetic mutations that made them fast. These cubs grew up to be great hunters because of their speed and were able to survive, reproduce and pass on the genetic sequences that made them fast |
| (C) One day a slow turtle just suddenly evolved into a fast cheetah | (D) Cheetahs ate fast animals like gazelles and the genetic material for being fast went into the cheetah's digestive system and caused cheetahs to be fast |

77

Worksheet 4

Date	Start time	End Time	Score

1. Thomas stirs 2 grams of salt into a cup of water. He then tries to get the salt back by evaporating the water. In this experiment, the mass of salt recovered would be the same as the initial mass because

(A) some salt evaporates with the water	(B) salt does not evaporate with water
(C) a chemical change occurred	(D) salt does not dissolve in water

2. A force of 5 N is required to increase the speed of a box from a rate of 1.0m/s to 3.0 m/s within 5 s along a level surface. What change would most likely require additional force to produce the same results?

(A) reduce the mass of the box	(B) increase the mass of the box
(C) make the surfaces of the box smooth	(D) make the surface of the floor smooth

3. Read the following table and answer the question

    Characteristics of Several Objects

Object	Mass (g)	Volume (cm^3)	Sink or Float
red ball	30.0	40.0	float
bottle	4.0	9.0	float
paper clip	1.0	0.4	sink
wooden block	12.8	16.0	float
magnet	2.2	0.2	sink
gold earring	1.5	1.7	float
ruler	14.0	12.0	sink
pink eraser	6.0	4.5	sink

Water mass = 20 g
Water volume = 20 cm^3

Which conclusion is best supported by the data above?

(A) Metal objects are more likely to float in water	(B) Color of the object determines if it sinks or floats
(C) shape of the object determines if it sinks or float	(D) object floats if its mass is less than its volume

4. What is the density of a 64-g iron cube that displaces 8 mL of water?

(A) 512 g/ml	(B) 32 g/ml
(C) 8 g/ml	(D) 4 g/ml

5. Motion growing stronger and stronger as time passes is known as:

| (A) Velocity | (B) Inertia |
| (C) Momentum | (D) Mass |

6. What property is measure by following tool in lab?

| (A) time | (B) volume |
| (C) temperature | (D) mass |

7. Two solutions are mixed and react to produce the solid precipitate AgCl. The chemical reaction is shown by the balanced chemical equation.

$AgNO_3 + NaCl \rightarrow AgCl + NaNO_3$

What happens to the total mass as the reaction takes place?

| (A) The mass remains constant | (B) The mass decreases. |
| (C) The mass increases. | (D) The mass first decreases and then increases. |

8. A piece of pine wood floats on the surface of a lake because the water exerts

| (A) an upward force equal to the weight of the wood. | (B) a downward force equal to the weight of the wood. |
| (C) an upward force equal to the weight of the displacement water. | (D) a downward force equal to the weight of the displacement water. |

9. How fast something is going is the

| (A) Velocity | (B) Inertia |
| (C) Momentum | (D) Acceleration |

10. A roller coaster car at the top of the hill is exhibiting

| (A) light energy | (B) Kinetic energy |
| (C) Momentum | (D) Potential energy |

11. Liam investigates the motion of a toy vehicle. Then he graphs 40 seconds of data from the investigation.

Motion of a Toy Vehicle

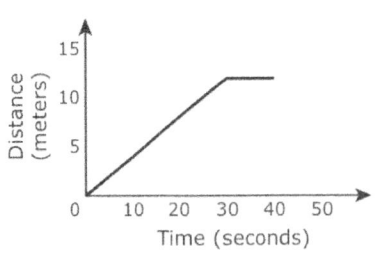

[Graph: Distance (meters) vs Time (seconds). Line rises linearly from (0,0) to about (30,12), then flat to (50,12).]

Which statement best describes the motion of the toy vehicle during the first 30 seconds of the investigation?

(A) The vehicle was traveling at a constant speed.	(B) The vehicle was accelerating at a constant rate.
(C) The speed of the vehicle was increasing.	(D) The acceleration of the vehicle was increasing.

12. Charles Darwin believed

(A) That reproduction has no role in evolution	(B) Individual organisms evolve within their lifetime
(C) Random mutations that make organisms more fit for its environment would survive and pass on genes	(D) Mutations happen in response to a need in the environment.

13. Sam heated 20 grams of liquid hydrogen peroxide until it was completely broken down into liquid water and oxygen gas. Which of this best describes the total mass of water and oxygen that was produced?

(A) more than 20 grams since heat was added	(B) 20 grams since no matter was added or removed
(C) less than 20 grams since oxygen gas is very light	(D) more than 20 grams since there are two new substances

14. Tim and Cole are pushing a cart, as shown below. The cart will move as if it were acted on by a single force with a magnitude of

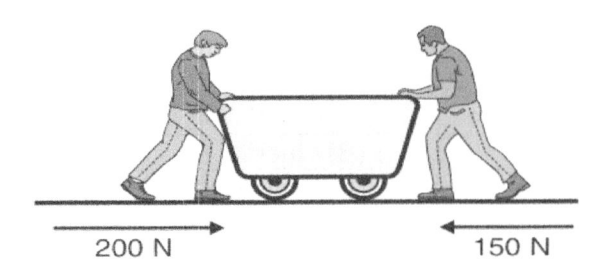

[Diagram: Two people pushing a cart from opposite sides. Left arrow labeled 200 N pointing right; right arrow labeled 150 N pointing left.]

(A) 50 N	(B) 150N
(C) 200N	(D) 350 N

15. What is the main function of an individual muscle cell?

(A) to grow and repair tissues	(B) to relax and contract tissues
(C) to support and protect organs	(D) to transmit and receive impulses

Worksheet 5

Date	Start time	End Time	Score

1. Four forces are acting on a box, as shown below. This box will increase in speed

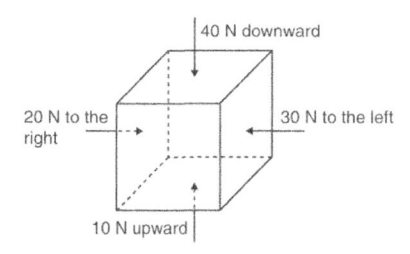

   (Diagram: box with 40 N downward, 20 N to the right, 30 N to the left, 10 N upward)

(A) downward and to the left.	(B) downward and to the right.
(C) upward and to the left.	(D) upward and to the right.

2. An experiment was preformed to test the effects of different types of fertilizers on the number of tomatoes produced by one type of tomato plant. What is the experimental (independent) variable in this investigation?

(A) color of plant	(B) type of fertilizer
(C) number of tomatoes	(D) type of plant

3. Which is the most basic unit of matter?

(A) compound	(B) element
(C) mixture	(D) molecule

4. What is the measure of the pull of gravity on an object

(A) inertia	(B) mass
(C) pressure	(D) weight

5. What is the force that resists motion between two surfaces that are in contact?

(A) Gravity	(B) Inertia
(C) Friction	(D) Velocity

6. What is natural selection?

(A) Organisms adapt to their surroundings as the need arises	(B) Organisms better adapted to their environment tend to survive, breed, and pass on the genetic traits.
(C) Populations of animals in nature, most often consist of genetic clones of each other	(D) Populations that become isolated from each other by adapting to different environmental niches can evolve into new species

7. Jose and Lin view two different cells under a microscope. They record their observations in the table shown.

Cell	Organelles Observed
1	Vacuoles Nucleus Cell Membrane
2	Vacuoles Nucleus Chloroplast Cell Wall

Based on the organelles observed, Jose and Lin determine that cell 2 is a plant cell because it has an organelle that —

(A) allows water to enter and exit the cell	(B) contains genetic information
(C) stores water and nutrients	(D) produces its own food

8. Ryan made a model using a globe and a flashlight. Which answer choice best explains the change from daytime to nighttime on Earth?

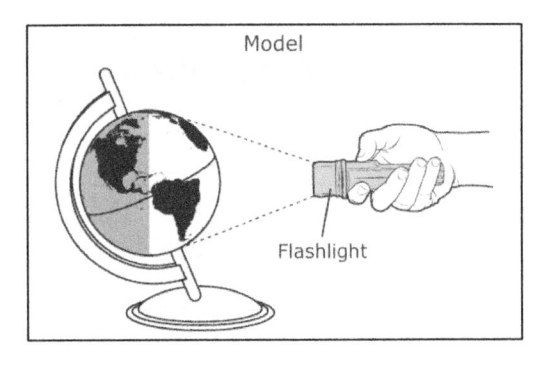

(A) The sun stops sending light to Earth at night.	(B) Earth moves farther away from the sun at night.
(C) The tilt of Earth causes less light to reach Earth at night.	(D) Earth rotates and causes different parts of Earth to experience night.

9. Major surface currents of the ocean are shown in the diagram

Ocean currents affect weather patterns by —

| (A) regulating when tides occur in coastal areas | (B) trapping heat at the equator to regulate the global climate |
| (C) distributing heat from the uneven absorption of solar energy | (D) increasing the rate of evaporation to transport water to areas experiencing droughts |

10. A toy car is at rest on the floor. Which statement describes the forces acting on the toy car?

| (A) The forces are balanced so motion occurs. | (B) The forces are balanced so no motion occurs. |
| (C) The forces are unbalanced so motion occurs. | (D) The forces are unbalanced so no motion occurs. |

11. In order for you to sit still on a bench in a park, what must be happening?

| (A) At least one force acting on the bench is balanced | (B) All of the forces acting on the bench are balanced |
| (C) The forces acting on the bench are unbalanced | (D) One of the forces acting on the bench has no mass |

12. Which statements correctly compare metals and nonmetals?

| (A) Metals tend to be good conductors of thermal energy. Nonmetals tend to be good insulators of thermal energy. | (B) Metals are dull and brittle. Nonmetals are shiny and malleable. |
| (C) Metals are good insulators of electricity. Nonmetals tend to be good conductors of electricity. | (D) Metals cannot be stretched into thin wires. Nonmetals can be stretched into thin wires. |

13. A ball is dropped from the top of a tall building. As the ball falls, the upward force of air resistance becomes equal to the downward pull of gravity. When these two forces become equal in magnitude, the ball will

| (A) flatten due to the forces | (B) fall at a constant speed |
| (C) continue to speed up | (D) slow to a stop |

14. Which is true about variation?

| (A) It is necessary for natural selection | (B) It is caused by mutations and sexual reproduction |
| (C) All populations have variations | (D) All of the above |

15. Which natural process results in offspring that are genetically identical to one parent?

| (A) asexual reproduction | (B) complete metamorphosis |
| (C) sexual reproduction | (D) incomplete metamorphosis |

Worksheet 6

Date	Start time	End Time	Score

1. An example of a balanced force is

(A) A rock going down a hill	(B) A person kicking a soccer ball
(C) A tug-of-war game in which no one wins	(D) A dog running

2. Use the diagram below to answer the question. What describes the event that occurred along line XY?

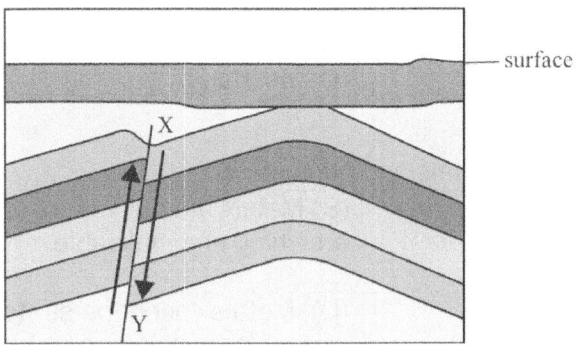

(A) erosion	(B) faulting
(C) sedimentary deposition	(D) volcanic eruption

3. Darwin's theory of natural selection, states that life in the wild is competitive, and organisms with the most beneficial traits will prosper. What is this commonly known as?

(A) Survival of the fittest	(B) Random mutations
(C) Best in running	(D) The Origin of the Species

4. Which determines the state of matter of a substance?

(A) density	(B) temperature
(C) volume	(D) weight

5. Use the pictures and table below to answer the question.

Bird Beaks and Diets

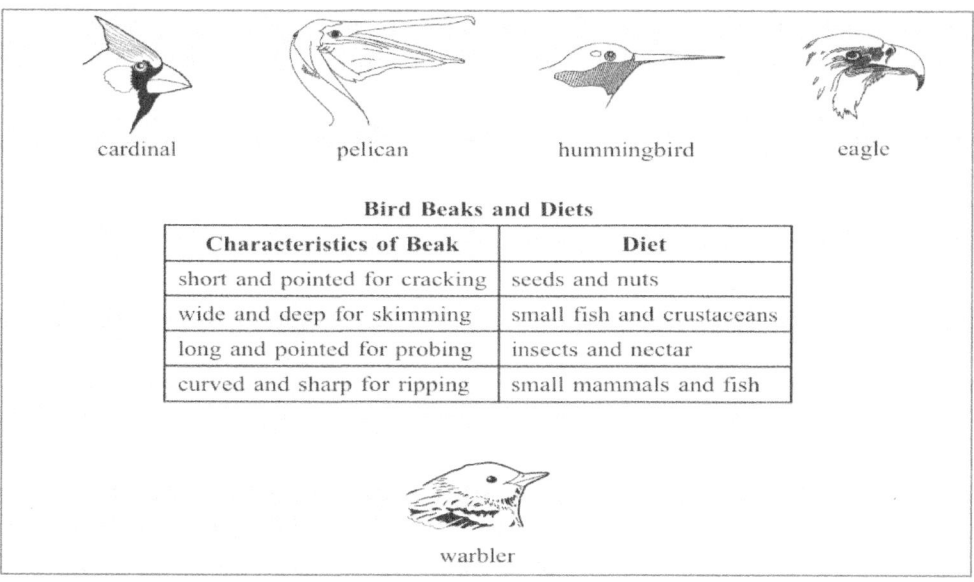

Characteristics of Beak	Diet
short and pointed for cracking	seeds and nuts
wide and deep for skimming	small fish and crustaceans
long and pointed for probing	insects and nectar
curved and sharp for ripping	small mammals and fish

What does a warbler MOST likely eat?

(A) fish and insects	(B) insects and nectar
(C) seeds and nuts	(D) small mammals and nuts

6. What is Earth's inner core made of?

(A) hot gases	(B) dense, solid metals
(C) partly-melted rock	(D) dense liquid materials

7. The graph below shows the speed of a vehicle over time. How far did the vehicle travel during the first two seconds?

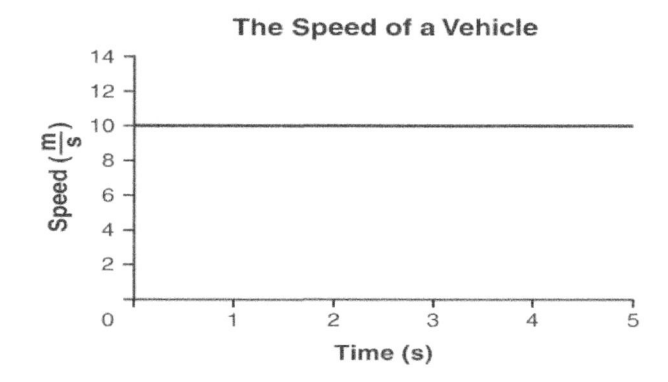

The Speed of a Vehicle

(A) 0.2 m	(B) 5m
(C) 10m	(D) 20m

85

8. One of the properties that makes copper, Cu, useful for electrical wiring is its ability to conduct electricity. Which other element is most likely to conduct electricity?

(A) Gold, Au	(B) Radon, Rn
(C) Bromine, Br	(D) Nitrogen, N

9. Unless a balanced force is applied, what will an object do naturally?

(A) Begin to change direction then stop	(B) Speed up until it reaches its maximum speed
(C) Slow down and stops	(D) Maintain its current speed and direction

10. The Sea-world amusement park added a new roller coaster.. A cart on a roller coaster approaches the highest point on the coaster. As the cart reaches the top, it slows down. Which statement best describes the energy of the roller coaster as it slows down while traveling to the top of the coaster?

(A) The cart gains both kinetic and potential energy.	(B) The cart gains kinetic energy and loses potential energy.
(C) The cart loses kinetic energy and gains potential energy.	(D) The cart loses both kinetic and potential energy.

11. All the individuals living in an area is known as

(A) Inheritance	(B) Descent with modification
(C) A population	(D) A group

12. A reflector helps people in cars see a bicycle when it is dark. How do bicycle reflectors work?

(A) They bounce light back from other sources.	(B) They are covered with paint that glows in the dark
(C) They are made of a special material that gives off its own light	(D) They are connected to batteries that allow them to produce their own light.

13. Which list has all terrestrial planets?

(A) Earth, Mars, Jupiter, Saturn	(B) Mercury, Venus, Earth, Mars
(C) Mars, Saturn, Jupiter, Neptune	(D) Jupiter, Saturn, Uranus, Neptune

14. The parent organisms of a rabbit are black and striped. They have 5 rabbits. Two are black, two are striped and one is grey. What is this an example of?

(A) Adaptive radiation	(B) Descent with modification
(C) Natural selection	(D) Survival of the fittest

15. The graph below shows how the position of an object changes over time. What is the speed of the object during the time interval from 4 seconds to 10 seconds?

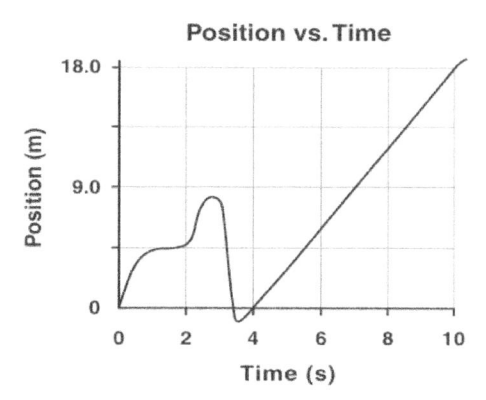

Position vs. Time

(A) 2 m/s	(B) 3 m/s
(C) 8 m/s	(D) 16 m/s

Worksheet 7

Date	Start time	End Time	Score

1. A partial grassland food web is shown.

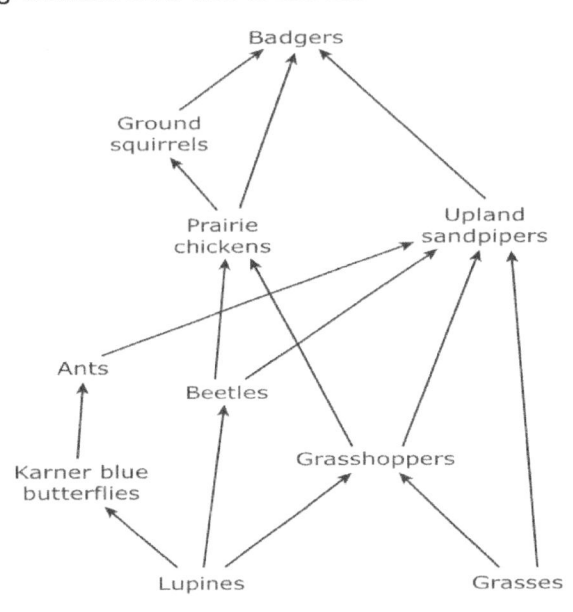

Which of the following best describes a relationship in this grassland?

(A) Badgers are top predators because they eat upland sandpipers and beetles.	(B) A producer–consumer relationship exists between lupines and ants.
(C) A predator–prey relationship exists between beetles and ground squirrels.	(D) Upland sandpipers are primary and secondary consumers because they eat grasses and grasshoppers.

2. Which of the following statements does NOT apply to Newton's Second Law of Motion?

(A) The acceleration of an object is dependent upon the net force acting upon the object	(B) The more mass an object has, the more force it takes to move it
(C) The force required to accelerate an object equals the object's mass times its acceleration	(D) If you apply different forces to to objects of the same size, they will accelerate equally

3. Which root system BEST helps a plant to survive in a dry environment with an underground water source?

(A) bulb root	(B) tap root
(C) runner	(D) tuber

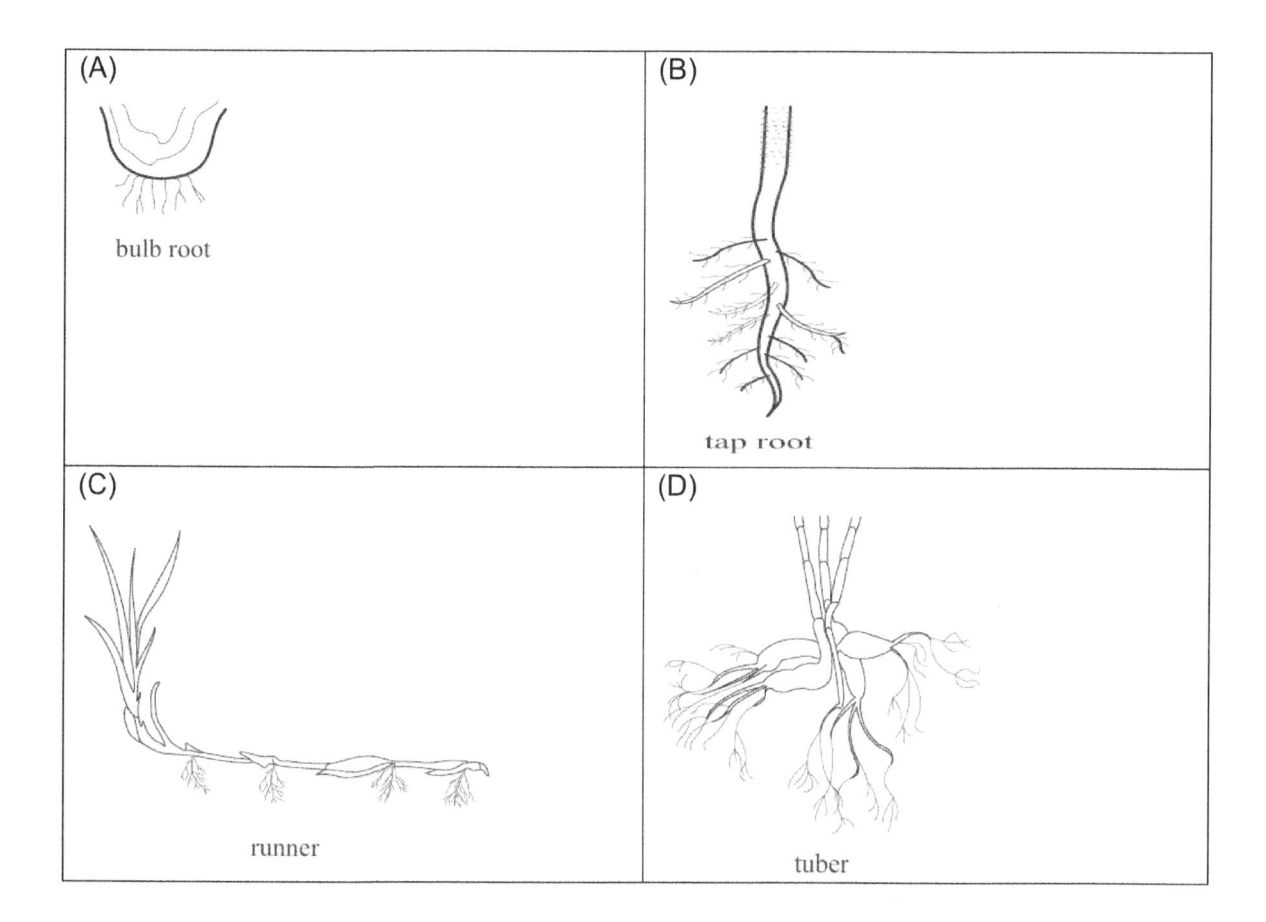

4. Why does an apple look red?

(A) Red light waves are reflected by the apple.	(B) Red light waves are absorbed by the apple.
(C) Red light waves are reflected by a student's eyes.	(D) Red light waves are absorbed by a student's eyes.

5. What is adaptive radiation?

(A) Developing adaptations to make oneself immune to radiation from the Sun	(B) Individuals adapt to their environment
(C) Behavioral adaptations	(D) As individual groups adapt to their different niches, they may evolve into distinct species

6. Which diagram shows the relative positions of Earth, the Moon and the Sun during a lunar eclipse?

89

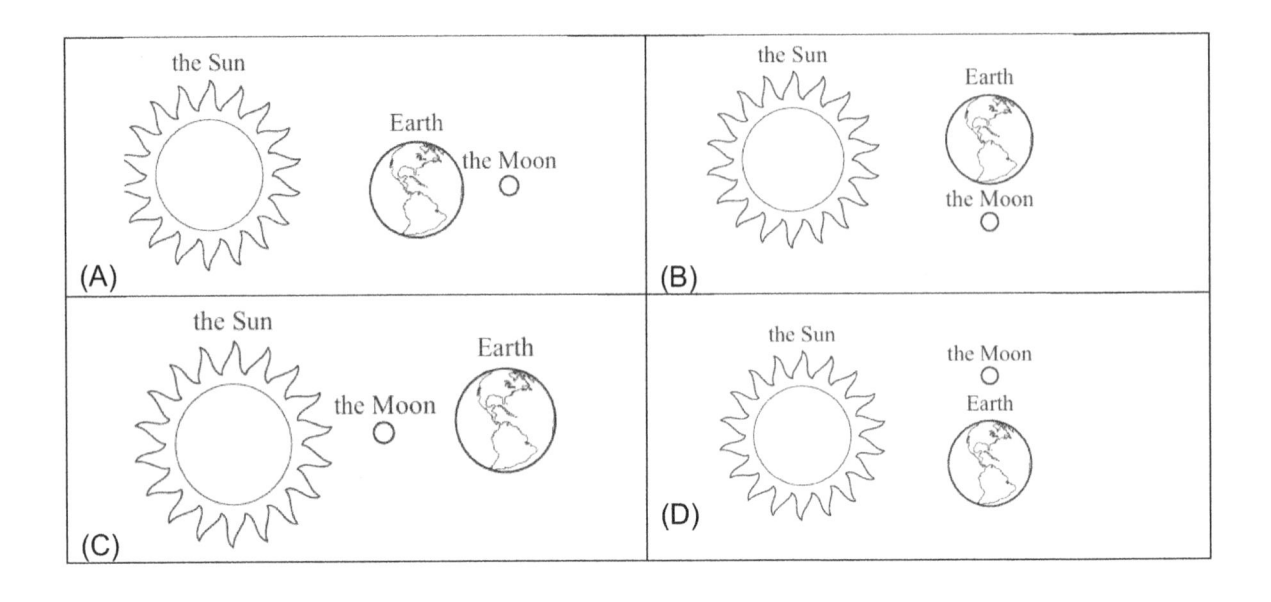

(A) the Sun, Earth, the Moon	(B) the Sun, Earth, the Moon
(C) the Sun, the Moon, Earth	(D) the Sun, the Moon, Earth

7. How would you explain the phenomena of a greater number of dark colored rats, than light colored rats, living on a dark rock?

(A) The rats know that being dark is safer, so they turn dark	(B) The dark-colored rats increased in population because they were smarter than the light-colored rats
(C) The dark-colored rats had an advantage over the light-colored rats on the dark background. The dark rats survived and were able to pass on their dark-color as a trait through reproduction	(D) The light-colored rats probably moved to a different rock, so they were not counted

8. Use the diagrams to answer the questions.

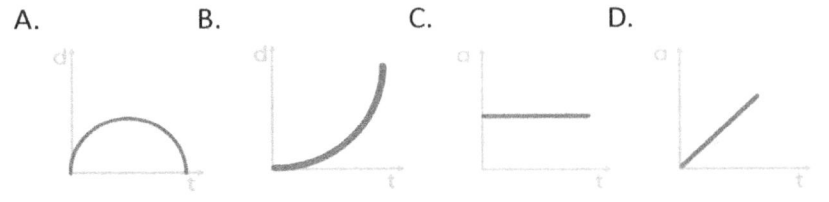

   A.   B.   C.   D.

Which graph represents an object that is not moving?

(A) A	(B) B
(C) C	(D) D

9. If the population of humans on earth continues to grow and we continue to use fossil fuels at the same rate we are using them now…

(A) We are likely to produce more fossil fuels	(B) We are likely to run out of fossil fuels and possibly damage our climate while doing so
(C) We are likely to find a way to make fossil fuels renewable	(D) We are likely to use fewer fossil fuels as our population continues to increase

10. Mia recorded the dates in May on which they observed a full moon and a last quarter moon.

Sunday	Monday	Tuesday	Wednesday	Thursday	Friday	Saturday
	01	02	03	04 Full	05	06
07	08	09	10	11 Last quarter	12	13
14	15	16	17	18	19	20
21	22	23	24	25	26	27
28	29	30	31			

On which date will they most likely be able to observe a new moon?

(A) May 13	(B) May 18
(C) May 25	(D) May 31

11. Absolute dating is also known as _____.

(A) Radiometric and radioactive dating	(B) Relative dating
(C) exact dating	(D) Rock Layer Exact Dating

12. What traits would be the fittest for a hot desert habitat?

(A) White colored feathers	(B) Methods for keeping cool, like being nocturnal
(C) Flippers for swimming	(D) A big fur coat

13. The beginning of autumn in North America is in September, but the beginning of autumn in South America is in March. The diagram shows the positions of Earth, the moon, and the sun on one day in September and one day in March.

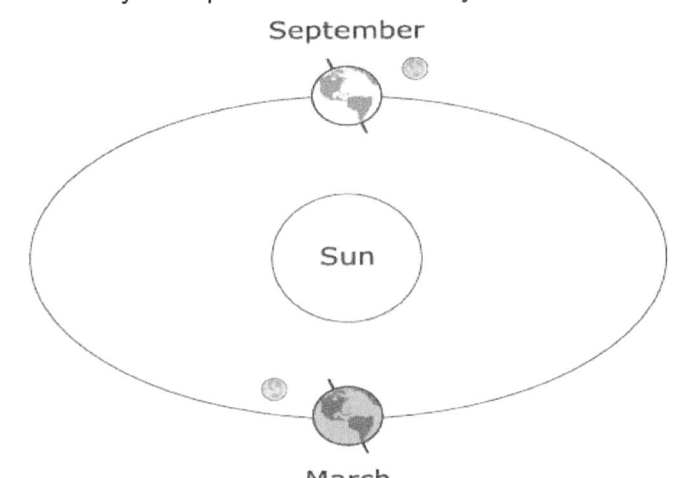

Why does autumn start in different months of the year in North America and South America?

(A) Earth's orbit around the sun is not a perfect circle.	(B) North America has a larger landmass than South America.
(C) The moon has a greater pull on South America than on North America.	(D) Earth's axis has a 23.5° tilt.

14. Which characteristic of motion could change without changing the velocity of an object?

(A) the speed	(B) the position
(C) the direction	(D) the acceleration

15. A scientist tests the effectiveness of a medicine. The medicine is administered to 2,500 volunteers who discontinue all other treatments. What is wrong with this experimental design?

(A) The experiment should include fewer volunteers	(B) The experiment should be administered in random dosages
(C) The experiment should include a group that does not take the medicine	(D) The experiment should allow the volunteers to continue other treatments.

Worksheet 8

Date	Start time	End Time	Score

1. Which is NOT an example of a symbiotic relationship?

(A) a tick biting a white-tailed deer	(B) a caterpillar changing into a butterfly
(C) a remora fish sticking to the shell of a sea turtle	(D) a clownfish living within the parts of a sea anemone

2. What is the title of the diagram shown below?

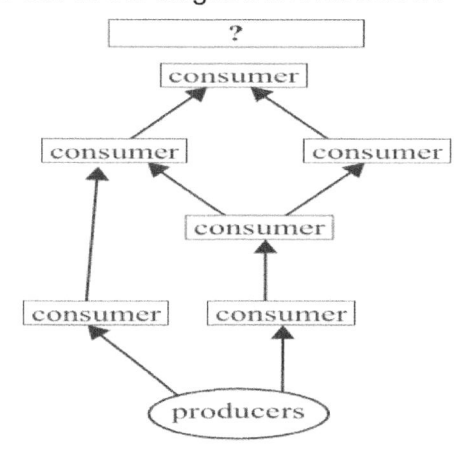

(A) Energy Pyramid	(B) Food Chain
(C) Water Cycle	(D) Food Web

3. The study of rock layers that is part of geology is known as_

(A) Layerology	(B) Stratigraphy
(C) Sedimentraphy	(D) Paleontology

4. Which of the following substances listed in the chart below, is made up of the most atoms?

Name	Chemical Formula
Carbonic acid	H_2CO_3
Nitric acid	HNO_3
Phosphoric acid	H_3PO_4
Sulfuric acid	H_2SO_4

(A) Carbonic acid	(B) Nitric acid
(C) Phosphoric acid	(D) Sulfuric acid

5. Use the diagrams to answer the questions

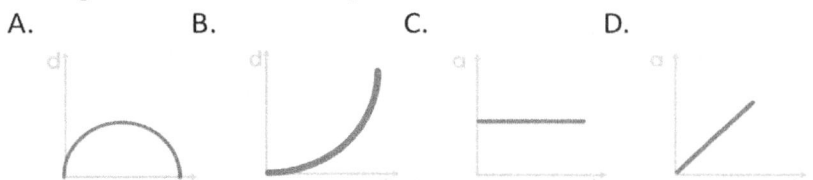

   A.   B.   C.   D.

   Which graph represents an object speeding up?

(A) A	(B) B
(C) C	(D) D

6. Which of the following represents the velocity of a moving object?

(A) 40	(B) 40 m North
(C) 40 m/s	(D) 40 m/s North

7. An ecosystem that is not sustainable can break down when a natural disaster occurs. This can lead to organisms in the ecosystem either leaving the area or dying off. Increased biodiversity results in a more sustainable ecosystem because —

(A) a greater number of plant species means that there is less barren land	(B) a greater variety of species present allows more organisms to adapt after changes occur
(C) the transition area between two ecosystems is narrower	(D) there are fewer species to be affected by environmental stresses

8. If an organism has a vestigial structure, the structure likely once had a function

(A) In a close relative	(B) In an embryo
(C) In an early ancestor	(D) In an unrelated organism

9. What characteristics must index fossils have?

(A) Long life span, lead isotopes	(B) 10 feet under ground and from animals, not plants
(C) small and round	(D) Recognizable, short life-span, wide distribution

10. Three different species of plants that live in the desert are shown.

Species X   Species Y   Species Z

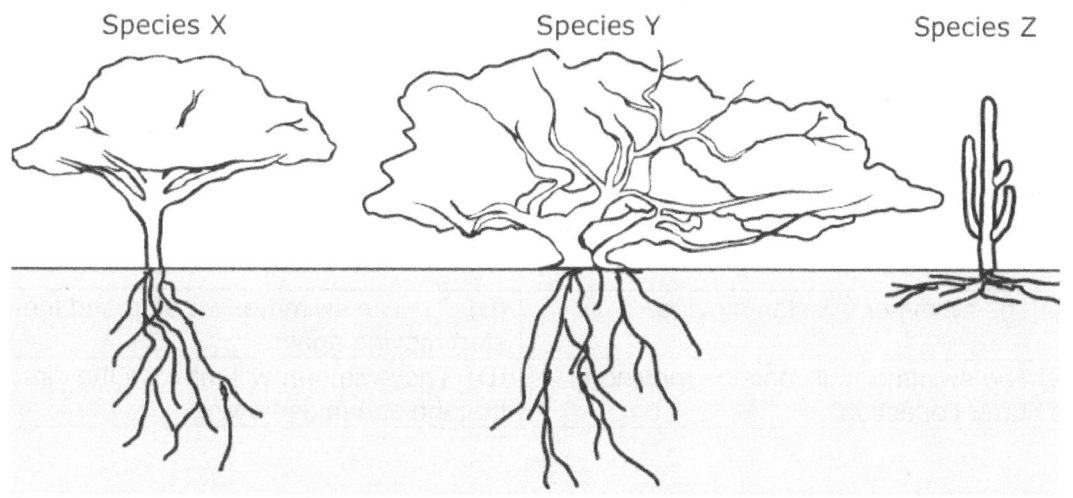

Species Z can successfully share the same environment with the other plants shown because species Z absorbs water —

(A) found deep underground, and species X absorbs water near the soil surface	(B) found deep underground, and species X absorbs water found deep underground
(C) near the soil surface, and species Y absorbs water near the soil surface	(D) near the soil surface, and species Y absorbs water found deep underground

11. A whale having hip bones is an example of a_____

(A) Homologous structure	(B) Analogous structure
(C) Vestigial structure	(D) All of these

12. Use the diagrams to answer the questions

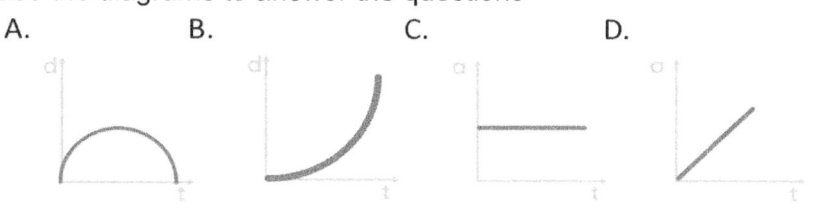

A.   B.   C.   D.

Which graph represents an object moving at a constant speed?

(A) A	(B) B
(C) C	(D) D

13. Which is true about absolute dating?

(A) It uses the half-life of isotopes to get the exact age of a rock or mineral	(B) The law of superposition is used to determine the absolute date of rocks
(C) Index fossils are compared to like	(D) It uses half-life to determine the length

| fossils in other strata to determine absolute age | of time an organism lived in various time periods |

14. A swimmer is swimming in a stream in the opposite direction the stream is flowing. The swimmer pushes against the water, so the water pushes the swimmer forward with 20 newtons of force. The water also exerts 15 newtons of resistive force against the swimmer. Which statement best describes the resulting motion of the swimmer?

(A) The swimmer will stop moving.	(B) The swimmer will stop and then start moving again.
(C) The swimmer will continue moving in its current direction.	(D) The swimmer will move in the direction that the stream is flowing.

15. Which of the following pieces of evolutionary evidence deals with comparing similar structures in various species?

(A) The Fossil record	(B) Comparative anatomy
(C) Comparing DNA	(D) Layers of the Earth

Worksheet 9

Date	Start time	End Time	Score

1. What is the original source of the energy released when fossil fuels are burned?

(A) decayed bacteria	(B) Earth's core
(C) nuclear	(D) solar

2. How much time is required for a bicycle to travel a distance of 100 m at an average speed of 2m/s?

(A) 0.02 s	(B) 50s
(C) 100s	(D) 200s

3. Use the pictures below to answer the question.

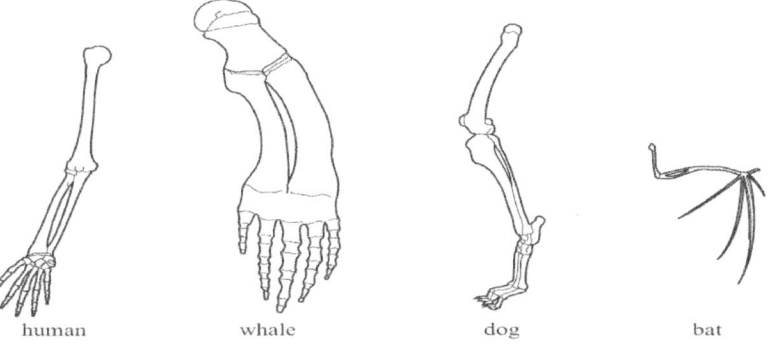

human   whale   dog   bat

What can be inferred from the bones in the pictures?

(A) all structural features are used to walk	(B) the organisms have similarities in skin features
(C) all structural features have a similar function	(D) the organisms have the same structural features

4. What is the average speed of the object in the graph below?

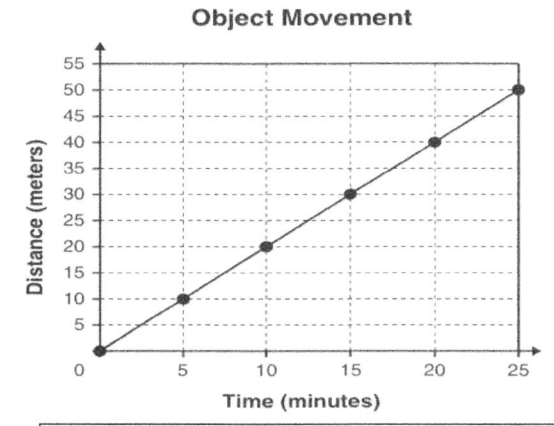

Object Movement

(A) 0.5 meters/minute	(B) 2 meters/minute
(C) 25 meters/minute	(D) 50 meters/minute

97

5. Use the diagrams to answer the questions

   A.   B.   C.   D.

   Which graph represents an object object that returns to its starting point?

(A) A	(B) B
(C) C	(D) D

6. Individuals with favorable traits survive, reproduce and pass on their traits to their offspring. What is this process called?

(A) Mutation	(B) Evolution
(C) Adaptation	(D) Natural selection

7. Ryan can run 9 kilometers in 1 hour. If he runs at that same average speed for 30 minutes, how far will Ryan travel?

(A) 18 km	(B) 9 km
(C) 4.5 km	(D) 3.3 km

8. What are two things you need to know if you are solving for speed?

(A) time and distance	(B) time and speed
(C) speed and distance	(D) distance and mass

9. A spring scale is pulled downward and readings are recorded.

   Data Table

Distance Pulled	Spring Scale Reading
1.0 cm	4 N
1.5 cm	6 N
2.0 cm	8 N
2.5 cm	10 N

   If the spring is pulled 3.5 cm, the spring scale should read

(A) 12 N	(B) 13 N
(C) 14 N	(D) 15 N

10. The temperature of a star determines the wavelength of visible light that is produced. The visible part of the electromagnetic spectrum is shown.

Light Spectrum

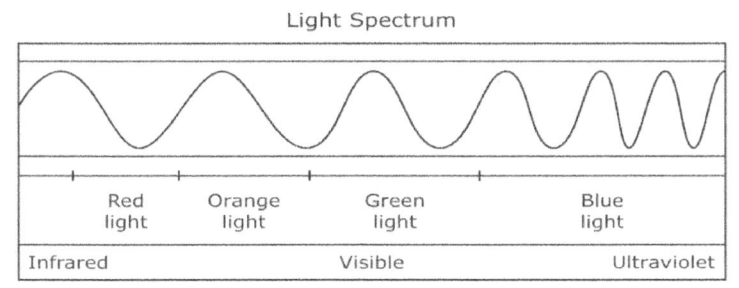

Red light	Orange light	Green light	Blue light
Infrared		Visible	Ultraviolet

Stars with the highest temperatures will emit most of their light at wavelengths that are near ____?

(A) red light	(B) orange light
(C) green light	(D) blue light

11. How old is the Earth?

(A) 5 billion years old	(B) 4.9 billion years old
(C) 4.6 billion years old	(D) 4.5 million years old

12. A bus travelled at 20 kilometers per hours for four hours. How far did the bus travel?

(A) 500 km	(B) 300 km
(C) 40 km	(D) 80 km

13. Students in Mr. Scott's class, mixed two liquids in a beaker and listed their observations.

Observations
Liquid 1 was colorless.
Liquid 2 was colorless.
The mixture of liquids 1 and 2 formed a colorless solution.
Small, solid particles formed and fell to the bottom of the beaker.

Based on these observations, which statement contains the best evidence that a chemical reaction occurred?

(A) There is a change in shape.	(B) There is a change in volume.
(C) The two liquids mix into a solution.	(D) The two liquids form a new substance.

14. What evidence do scientists use to determine the age of the Earth?

(A) Index fossils	(B) Earth strata
(C) Radioactive Dating	(D) All of the options are correct

15. Bat wings and bird wings are an example of

(A) Homologous structures	(B) Analogous structures
(C) Vestigial structures	(D) All of these

Worksheet 10

Date	Start time	End Time	Score

1. Data from an experiment are presented below. The slope of the graph represents what characteristic of an object?

    Experimental Data

Distance	Time
5 cm	0.2 s
15 cm	0.4 s
25 cm	0.6 s
35 cm	0.8 s

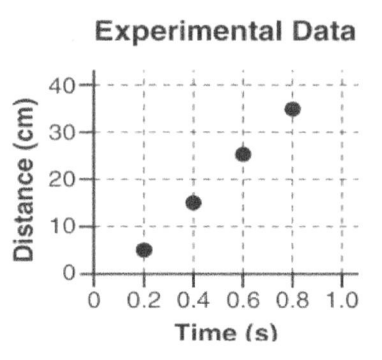

(A) displacement	(B) force
(C) speed	(D) inertia

2. A galaxy is best described as a cluster of

(A) hundreds of stars.	(B) thousands of stars
(C) millions of stars.	(D) billions of stars

3. Why can you get a shock if your touch a metal doorknob after picking up a woolen coat ?

(A) You have gained electrons the doorknob has no electrons	(B) You have lost electrons, the doorknob has many electrons
(C) You have gained protons and the doorknob has gained electrons	(D) You have gained neutrons, the doorknob has last neutrons

4. Humans, birds, dolphins, and lizards all have similar forearm bones. What is the reason for this?.

(A) They live in similar environments	(B) function of these bones is the same in all animals
(C) They have a common ancestor	(D) They are analogous

5. Ryan is holding a box with a steel ball. The steel ball is at one end of a box that is moving forward as shown. The box suddenly stops.

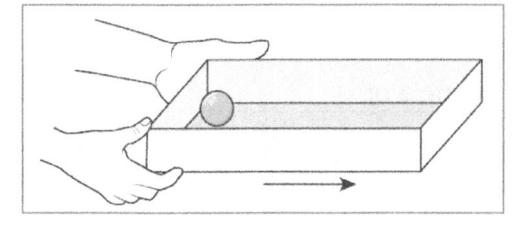

100

According to Newton's first law, what happens to the steel ball just after the box stops?

(A) the ball continues rolling forward at the same speed, because of friction	(B) the ball rolls forward at an increased speed, because of friction
(C) Because of inertia, the ball continues rolling forward at the same speed.	(D) Because of inertia, the ball rolls forward at an increased speed.

6. Students build a circuit. The circuit has wires that connect a battery to a switch and a fan. Which energy transformations happen when the students close the circuit and the blades of the fan begin to spin?

(A) Chemical to electrical to mechanical	(B) Electrical to chemical to mechanical
(C) Chemical to mechanical to electrical	(D) Mechanical to electrical to chemical

7. Max drew atomic models of four elements.

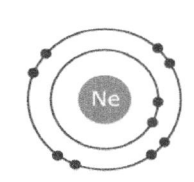

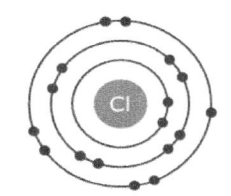

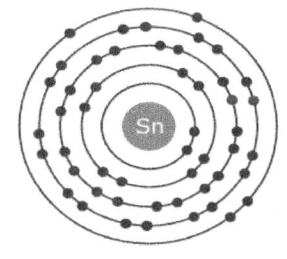

Based on these drawings, which element is the least reactive?

(A) Neon, because it has two energy levels with eight electrons in the second level	(B) Chlorine, because it has three energy levels with seven electrons in the third level
(C) Gallium, because it has four energy levels with three electrons in the fourth level	(D) Tin, because it has five energy levels with four electrons in the fifth level

8. What do the similarities between ancient organisms and modern organisms tell us?

(A) Ancient organisms are still around	(B) There is no relationship between modern organism and ancient organism
(C) There may be an evolutionary connection between the ancient organisms and modern organisms	(D) All of these

9. Which of these time periods lasted the longest?

(A) Precambrian Time	(B) Paleozoic Era
(C) Mesozoic Era	(D) Cenozoic

10. Two balloons are rubbed with a piece of wool. What will happen if the two balloons are brought close to each other?

(A) The balloons will repel each other	(B) The balloons will attract each other
(C) The balloons will pop	(D) The Balloons will become magnetized

11. A student divides several cubes into two groups, based on whether or not each cube can float in water. What property is the student using to classify the cubes?

(A) weight	(B) density
(C) conductivity	(D) mass

12. Immediately after a forest fire, the primary consumers in the area will compete most for which biotic factor?

(A) Food	(B) Space
(C) Oxygen	(D) Sunlight

13. Dinosaurs ruled the Earth in what period?

(A) Precambrian Time	(B) Paleozoic Era
(C) Mesozoic Era	(D) Cenozoic

14. Patterns in the fossil record

(A) Provide support for the theory of evolution	(B) Do not have any sequence to them
(C) Show that most organisms have not changed over the last million years	(D) Show us that while landforms might change, climate has remained same over millions of years

15. What type of charges attract?

(A) Positive and Negative	(B) Negative and Negative
(C) Neutral and negative	(D) Positive and Positive

Worksheet 11

Date	Start time	End Time	Score

1. In a comparison of metals to nonmetals, metals tend to have

(A) lower melting points and greater conductivity than nonmetals.	(B) lower conductivity and lower density than nonmetals.
(C) higher density and lower melting points than nonmetals.	(D) greater conductivity and higher melting points than nonmetals.

2. To express the distance between the Milky Way galaxy and other galaxies, the most appropriate unit of measurement is the

(A) meter	(B) kilometer
(C) light-year.	(D) astronomical unit

3. What charge does a proton have?

(A) Negative	(B) no charge
(C) Positive	(D) sometimes positive sometimes negative

4. What controls the orbits of objects in our solar system?

(A) Speed and light	(B) Inertia and gravity
(C) Gravity and speed	(D) Momentum and inertia

5. In what geological era are we currently living?

(A) Precambrian Time	(B) Paleozoic Era
(C) Mesozoic Era	(D) Cenozoic

6. What factors does the strength of the force of gravity depend on?

(A) The masses of the objects and their speed	(B) The mass and weight of the objects
(C) The masses of the objects and the distance between them	(D) The length of the object and its speed

7. When the moon blocks the Sun's light, a _____ eclipse occurs

(A) Solar	(B) Lunar
(C) Polaris	(D) Interstellar

8. What is static discharge?

(A) Electrons moving quickly from one object to another in order to restore charge balance	(B) Protons moving from one object to another
(C) Electrons moving to create charge imbalance	(D) A Tubelight coming on when a switch is turned

9. In an area of sedimentary rocks, the bottom rocks show organisms that lived in the ocean. The land is currently on a mountain top. What can we conclude from this information?

(A) The ocean once covered this area	(B) The Earth's surface has changed over time
(C) This change was probably a gradual change	(D) All the options are true

10. Below is the food web. What do the birds in this food web feed on?

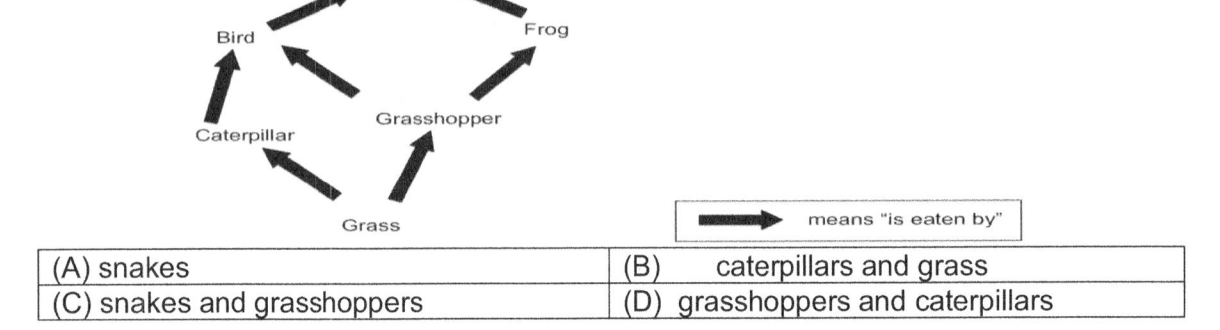

(A) snakes	(B) caterpillars and grass
(C) snakes and grasshoppers	(D) grasshoppers and caterpillars

11. Scientists think that temperatures on Earth are increasing. This is called the "Greenhouse Effect". Which gas contributes most to the increasing temperature on Earth?

(A) carbon dioxide	(B) oxygen
(C) nitrogen	(D) helium

12. When the moon passes through the Earth's shadow, a _____ eclipse occurs.

(A) Solar	(B) Lunar
(C) Polaris	(D) interstellar

13. An energy field can be demonstrated through (Select all that apply)

(A) Magnets attracting certain objects	(B) drinking soda
(C) Static electricity making objects move	(D) Riding a car

14. Which of the following sets contains only objects that shine as a result of reflected light?

(A) moons, planets, and comets	(B) moons, comets, and stars
(C) planets, stars, and comets	(D) planets, stars, and moons

15. The moon has phases where it seems to change shape in the sky. A solar eclipse occurs during what moon phase

(A) Full moon	(B) Waning crescent
(C) Waxing crescent	(D) New moon

Worksheet 12

Date	Start time	End Time	Score

1. Which class of elements best conducts electricity?

(A) metals	(B) nonmetals
(C) semimetals	(D) noble (inert) gases

2. An object composed mainly of ice is orbiting the Sun in an elliptical path. This object is most likely

(A) planet	(B) asteroid
(C) meteor.	(D) comet

3. Why do we have seasons? (Select all the answers that are true)

(A) Earth is closer to the Sun in summer than winter	(B) We receive direct and indirect sunlight
(C) Earth is farther from the Sun in winter than summer	(D) The Earth is tilted

4. Which of the following is true about an electromagnet?

(A) Their strength is set and there is not much you can do to adjust the strength	(B) They do not produce an energy field
(C) They can be turned on and off by opening the electrical circuit	(D) none

5. What is a living fossil?

(A) An organism that was once a fossil come back to life	(B) An organism that has changed very little and can still be found on Earth today
(C) A fossilized plant	(D) A fossil produced while the organism was still alive

6. As the Earth revolves around the Sun, the Earth's axis is pointed at...

(A) Deneb	(B) Thuban
(C) Polaris	(D) Vega

7. After playing football Danny found his shirt was wet from sweating (perspiring). What is the main reason why people sweat?

(A) it helps keep their bodies cool	(B) so they will be thirsty and drink more
(C) it gets rid of extra water from their bodies	(D) it gets rid of extra salt from their bodies

8. What happens when two North poles of magnets are placed together?

(A) They will attract to each other	(B) They cancel each other out
(C) The strength of the magnet is doubled	(D) They will repel away from each other

9. What season in the southern hemisphere experiencing when the northern hemisphere leaning towards the Sun?

(A) Summer	(B) Fall
(C) Spring	(D) Winter

10. Copper (Cu) reacts with oxygen (O) to form copper oxide (CuO). The properties of CuO are most likely

(A) different from copper or oxygen.	(B) similar to both copper and oxygen
(C) similar only to copper	(D) similar only to oxygen

11. The table below shows the atomic mass of four stable calcium (Ca) isotopes. What characteristic is different in each isotope?

Isotope	Atomic Mass
Ca–40	40
Ca–42	42
Ca–43	43
Ca–44	44

(A) position in the periodic table of the elements	(B) the net charge of the nucleus
(C) the mass of the protons in the nucleus	(D) the number of neutrons in the nucleus

12. Magnets can be used in industry in the following areas. (check all that apply)

(A) Medicine	(B) Security
(C) Computers	(D) Banks and credit cards

13. What is an index fossil?

(A) Index fossils are fossils that are found in the rock layers of only one geologic age	(B) Index fossils are fossils that are of living fossils
(C) Index fossils are whole body fossils of animals caught in amber	(D) Index fossils show up in every layer from all time periods

14. The direction of the outside magnetic field is from

(A) Front to back	(B) south pole to north pole
(C) Inside to outside of the magnet	(D) north pole to south pole

15. Which of the following compounds is most likely to be part of living organisms?

(A) $C_6H_{12}O_6$	(B) BF_3
(C) $MoCl_2$	(D) CsI

Worksheet 13

Date	Start time	End Time	Score

1. A diagram of the periodic table of the elements is shown below.

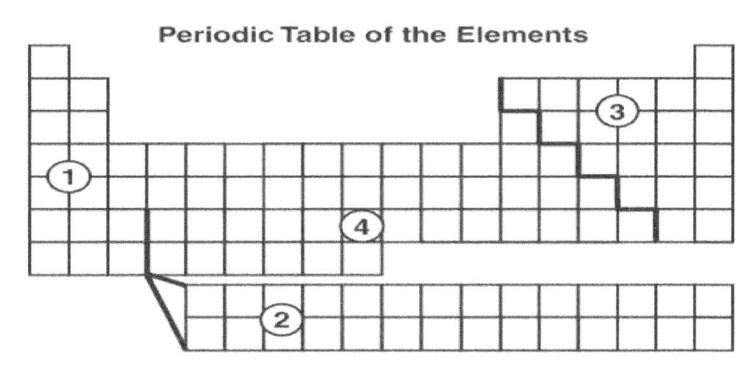

   In which region of the table would nonmetals be found?

(A) 1	(B) 2
(C) 3	(D) 4

2. The following equations represent chemical reactions.

1	$2Na + 2H_2O \rightarrow NaOH + H_2$
2	$H_2 + O_2 \rightarrow H_2O$
3	$Mg + Cl_2 \rightarrow MgCl_2$
4	$NaOH + MgCl_2 \rightarrow NaCl + MgOH$

   Which equation shows that the total mass during a chemical reaction stays the same?

(A) 3	(B) 2
(C) 1	(D) 4

3. Which of the following is the best conductor of electricity?

(A) Rubber	(B) Glass
(C) Copper	(D) Wood

4. Which force is responsible for keeping planets in orbit around the sun?

(A) Electromagnetic force	(B) Gravitational force
(C) Nuclear force	(D) Frictional force

5. The strength of a magnetic field can be measured

(A) Using a Measuring tape	(B) Observing how many items of a particular type are picked up
(C) By seeing if it will attract to pennies	(D) By putting the magnet on a bathroom scale to test its weight

6. The diagram shows the different layers of rocks in a cliff

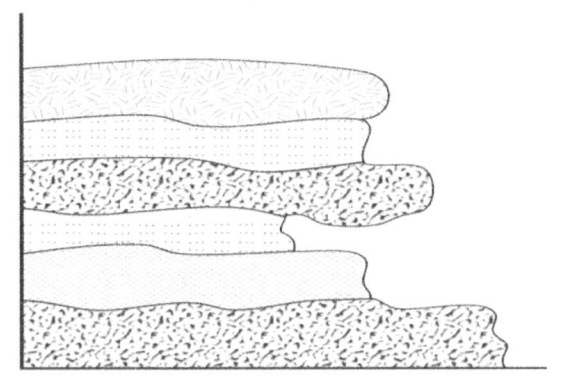

Which type of rock is most resistant to weathering?

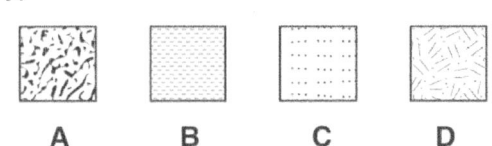

(A)	A	(B)	B
(C)	C	(D)	D

7. What is our main source of heat on Earth?

(A) Geothermal	(B) Natural Gas
(C) Mars	(D) Sun

8. All matter is made up of

(A) Cells	(B) Atoms
(C) Amino acids	(D) Dust

9. The shape of the Earth's orbit is

(A) rectangular	(B) circular
(C) elliptical	(D) a straight line

10. The full moon is followed by which major lunar phase?

(A) Waning crescent	(B) Waxing crescent
(C) Waxing gibbous	(D) Waning gibbous

11. The electrons in an atom

(A) Sometimes convert to protons	(B) Are very stable and consistent within the atom
(C) Can sometimes move to another surface through friction	(D) Sometimes convert to neutrons

12. What causes a static lightning discharge?

(A) The buildup of electrical charges in	(B) The movement of tectonic plates

clouds	
(C) The collision of two warm air masses	(D) The evaporation of water from the Earth's surface

13. What is the Law of Superposition?

(A) The larger the layer the older it is	(B) Older layers are at the top
(C) The layer on the bottom is the oldest	(D) Igneous rocks are always older than sedimentary rocks

14. Which of the following elements is best able to combine with itself and hydrogen (H) to form large molecules?

(A) sodium (Na)	(B) lithium (Li)
(C) sulfur (S)	(D) carbon (C)

15. What does the strength of the force of gravity depend on?

(A) The masses of the objects and their speed	(B) The masses of the objects and the distance between them
(C) The mass and weight of the objects	(D) The length of the object and its speed

Worksheet 14

Date	Start time	End Time	Score

1. What is the name of the indicated atom in the acetic acid molecule shown below?

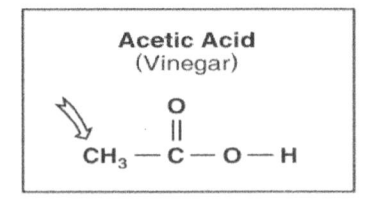

    Acetic Acid (Vinegar)
    $$CH_3-C(=O)-O-H$$

(A) carbon	(B) calcium
(C) chromium	(D) copper

2. What is the definition of inertia?

(A) The force of a push or a pull on an object	(B) The force pulling us towards the Earth
(C) increasing force because of increased mass of an object	(D) The tendency of an object to resist change in motion

3. Which of the following forms of energy is released or absorbed in most chemical reactions?

(A) light energy	(B) electrical energy
(C) sound energy	(D) heat energy

4. Fossilized nests, burrows, feces and footprints are what type of fossil?

(A) Mold Fossil	(B) Cast Fossil
(C) Trace Fossil	(D) True Form Fossil

5. How long does it take fossils to form?

(A) 1000 Days	(B) About 100 years
(C) Thousands of years	(D) Millions of years

6. A magnetic field is made up of

(A) Positive and negative charges	(B) agnetic domains
(C) Magnetic poles	(D) Static flux

7. In Mr Lin's Sceince class, group of students doing egg drop experiment, each group must design a container that will keep the egg from breaking when it is dropped 10 feet. What scientific principles will naturally be part of the constraints? (select all that apply)

(A) Gravity	(B) Insulators
(C) Conductors	(D) Analog signals

110

8. As a sample of water turns to ice,

| (A) new molecules are formed. | (B) the mass of the sample is increased |
| (C) the arrangement of the molecules changes | (D) energy is absorbed by the molecules |

9. In a balloon rocket experiment, each group must design a rocket that will travel the farthest distance when propelled by air from an inflated balloon. What scientific principles will naturally be part of the constraints? (select all that apply)

| (A) Air pressure | (B) Friction |
| (C) Magnetism | (D) Gravity |

10. What controls the orbits of objects in our solar system?

| (A) Speed and light | (B) Inertia and gravity |
| (C) Gravity and speed | (D) Momentum and inertia |

11. What is a true form fossil?

| (A) A fossil that is made from a footprint | (B) fossil made from the actual organism itself |
| (C) A fossilized impression | (D) A filled-in version of a fossilized impression |

12. When south poles of two bar magnets are brought close together, there will be____.

| (A) A force of repulsion | (B) A force of attraction |
| (C) An upward force | (D) No forces |

13. What do the elements sulfur (S), nitrogen (N), phosphorus (P), and bromine (Br) have in common?

| (A) They are noble (inert) gases | (B) They are nonmetals |
| (C) They have the same thermal conductivity | (D) They have the same number of protons |

14. What characteristic of carbon (C) makes it essential to living organisms?

| (A) Carbon forms crystal structures under certain conditions. | (B) Carbon can exist as a solid, liquid, or gas. |
| (C) Carbon bonds in many ways with itself to form chains. | (D) Carbon exists in radioactive forms. |

15. Our solar system is part of the

| (A) Andromeda Galaxy | (B) Milky Way Galaxy |
| (C) Magellan Galaxy | (D) Perseus Galaxy |

Worksheet 15

Date	Start time	End Time	Score

1. Iron oxides, such as rust, form when iron metal reacts with oxygen in the air. What are the chemical symbols for the two elements found in iron oxide?

(A) I and O	(B) Ir and O
(C) Fe and O	(D) Pb and O

2. Which mutation is most likely to provide a benefit to the organism?

(A) A genetic disease	(B) A change in coloration that may provide camouflage in the environment
(C) An inability to conserve water in a plant	(D) Longer tail on a monkey

3. Ms. Hong's class did an experiment with litmus test and created following table.

Body Fluid	pH	red litmus	blue litmus
Blood	7.4	turns blue	no change
Bile	8.2	turns blue	no change
Saliva	6.8	no change	turns red
Gastric Juice	1.7	no change	turns red

These data indicate that gastric juice is

(A) very acidic	(B) very basic.
(C) positively charged	(D) negatively charged

4. What is the shape of the Milky Way Galaxy?

(A) square	(B) oblong
(C) spiral	(D) irregular

5. The part of the animal that can form a fossil is

(A) Hard parts, like teeth and bones	(B) Soft parts like stomach and blood
(C) The brain	(D) Only the bones

6. The new moon is followed by which major lunar phase?

(A) Waning crescent	(B) Waxing crescent
(C) Waning gibbous	(D) Waxing gibbous

7. Genes are located

(A) In the cell membrane	(B) In chromosomes
(C) In chloroplasts	(D) None option is correct

8. What are the four types of fossils?

(A) trace, hard, soft, shells	(B) mold, trace, true form, and cast
(C) mold, true form, false form, bones	(D) none

9. How many stars are estimated to be in the Milky Way Galaxy?

(A) At least 100 billion	(B) Less than 100,000
(C) About 10000	(D) About 100 million

10. Which is NOT true of static electricity?

(A) an imbalance of electric charges within or on the surface of a material or between materials occurs	(B) An invisible electric field exists
(C) The charge can be transferred from one object to another	(D) Must travel through a circuit

11. . In order to see the phases of the moon, what space objects play a role?

(A) Asteroids	(B) Stars and comets
(C) Earth, Sun and moon	(D) Planets of the solar system

12. What type of rock are fossils found in?

(A) Metamorphic	(B) Igneous
(C) Sedimentary	(D) None

13. Mutations to genes

(A) Create a temporary change in the DNA sequence	(B) Does not make much difference to DNA structure
(C) are a structural change to a gene's DNA sequence	(D) Are always harmful

14. What is the mechanism that allows us to see light from the moon?

(A) Reflected light	(B) Refracted light
(C) The moon's own light	(D) Light from the Earth

15. Using static electricity you can push an empty aluminum can without touching it. This is evidence of a _____

(A) Magnetic force	(B) Static electric field
(C) Neutral charges	(D) Opposite poles

Performance Tasks
And
Constructed-Response Questions

Worksheet 1

1. In diagram below, describe the relationship between distance and force of gravity.

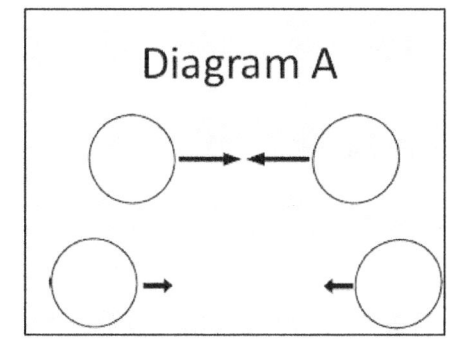

   Diagram A

2. What is the difference between mass and weight?

3. What does diagram below show you about the relationship of mass and the force of gravity

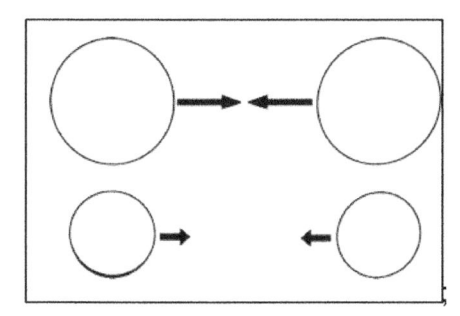

115

4. Why do astronauts feel weightless in space?

5. What is the gravitational force acting on a 10 kg object on Earth?

Worksheet 2

1. Describe what happens if you are riding a skateboard and hit something (like a curb) with the front wheels.

2. Use one of Newton's Laws to explain why you should wear seatbelts?

3. Explain what inertia is. Which of Newton's laws is connected to the concept of inertia?

4. Unbalanced forces cause acceleration. In what direction is the acceleration?

5. How is mass related to inertia? Would it take more force to move a light box or a heavy box?

Worksheet 3

1. How are Artificial and Natural selection similar?

2. A dolphin flipper and a human hand have similar bone structures. How do you think they developed into their present form?

Question 3 and 4 are related to following description

In England before the industrial revolution, peppered moths were mainly white with black speckles, but a small group within the population had a genetic mutation that caused them to appear dark gray. After industrialization, the increase in air pollution caused tree bark to darken Eventually, the lighter-colored peppered moths became less common than the dark-gray moths

3. Identify one possible advantage dark-gray peppered moths had over the lighter-colored moths after the industrial revolution.

4. In the above question: Predict what will most likely happen to the coloration of peppered moths as pollution control measures increase in England

5. How can natural selection affect a population's genetic diversity?

Worksheet 4

Question 1 and 2 are based on following description

A student is testing if the mass of a balloon rocket affects how far it travels on a string by attaching metal washers to the balloon. The student measures the initial circumference of the balloon at the beginning of each trial.

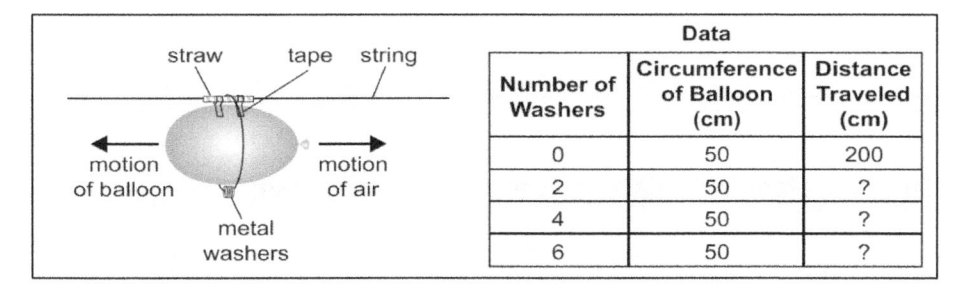

Number of Washers	Circumference of Balloon (cm)	Distance Traveled (cm)
0	50	200
2	50	?
4	50	?
6	50	?

1. Predict the general relationship between the distance the balloon rocket would likely travel and the number of washers it carries.

2. In a second investigation the student uses no washers but changes the balloon's circumference. Predict the general relationship between the distance the balloon rocket would likely travel and the circumference of the balloon

3. What factors determine the distance a rocket can travel?

4. How does Newton's Third Law of Motion apply to a rocket?

5. How does friction affect the distance a moving object travels?

119

Worksheet 5

1. Why do plant cells have a cell wall and animal cells do not?

2. Compare and contrast plant and animal cells using a Venn diagram.

3. What is the function of the cell membrane and nucleus in cell?

4. How do chloroplasts function in plant cells?

5. How do vacuoles differ in plant and animal cells?

Worksheet 6

The image below shows some selected properties of Earth's atmosphere.

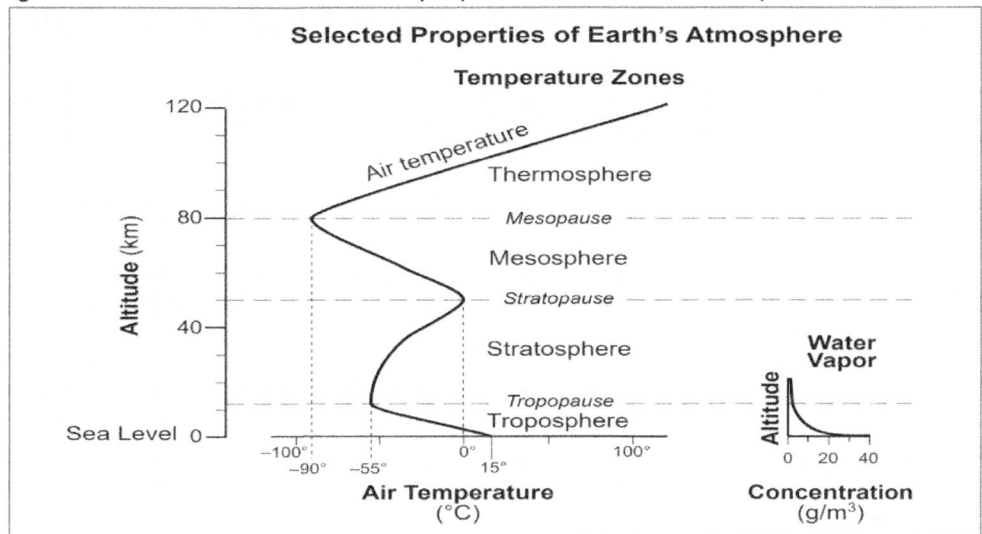

Selected Properties of Earth's Atmosphere

[Diagram showing Temperature Zones with altitude (km) vs. Air Temperature (°C): Troposphere, Tropopause, Stratosphere, Stratopause, Mesosphere, Mesopause, Thermosphere. Reference temperatures marked: −100°, −90°, −55°, 0°, 15°, 100°. Separate Water Vapor graph showing Concentration (g/m³) vs. Altitude, with values 0, 20, 40.]

1. Identify the air temperature at the stratopause and the mesopause.
    Stratopause _____ °C   Mesopause _____ °C

2. State the general relationship between water vapor concentration and altitude within the troposphere.

3. Why does temperature change with altitude in the atmosphere?

4. What are the characteristics of the thermosphere?

5. How does the ozone layer protect life on Earth?

121

Worksheet 7

A student conducted an experiment to see if a popular brand of plant food had any effect on bean plants growing in sand. Ten plants were started from seed. Each seed was planted in a small container filled with sand. Plant food was added to the sand in only five of the containers. All other physical factors were kept the same for all ten plants. The experiment continued for 35 days. The student kept a journal during the experiment. Three of the entries are shown in the table below.

Day	Entry
15	During the first 15 days, the plants all looked the same. There was no difference between the plant food group and the other group without plant food.
30	Observed the plants today. The five seeds given plant food were all at least 5 cm taller than the group without plant food. They also had at least two more leaves than the group without plant food. Some of the leaves on the group without plant food were yellowish.
35	My experiment shows that bean plant growth is increased by adding plant food to sand.

1. Explain why plant food was not given to five of the ten seeds in this experiment.

2. Identify the independent (manipulated) variable.

3. Describe one piece of evidence from the entries in the student's journal that would support the conclusion made on day 35.

122

Worksheet 8

The diagram below represents two bar magnets labeled A and B. They are positioned close enough to attract or repel each other.

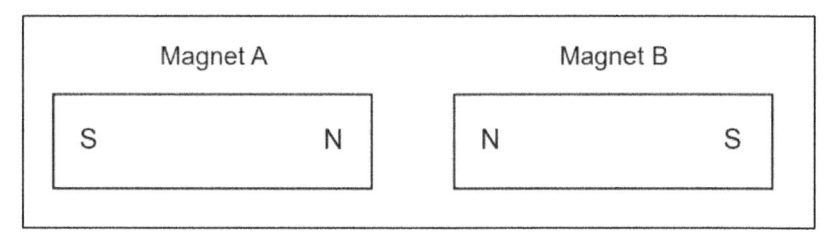

Magnet A	Magnet B
S N	N S

1. State whether the two magnets will attract or repel each other and explain why this will occur.
   - Attract or Repel: _____
   - Explanation

2. How do the poles of a magnet interact with each other?

3. How can you make a simple electromagnet?

4. How does the Earth's magnetic field affect compasses?

5. What is magnetic induction?

Worksheet 9

The diagram below represents two identical carts, A and B, each with a mass of 4 kilograms (kg). An object with a mass of 2 kg is placed on cart B. An equal force of 8 newtons (N) is used to pull each cart over the same surface.

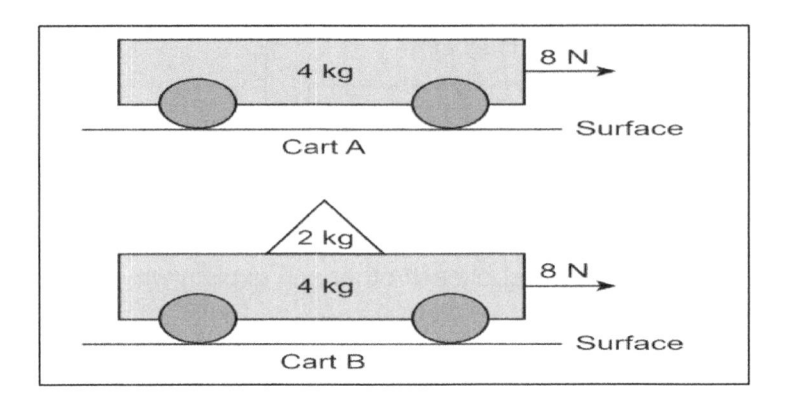

1. Using the equation below, calculate the acceleration of cart A, in meters per second squared

    $$\text{Acceleration} = \frac{\text{Force}}{\text{Mass}}$$

    Answer _____

2. Explain why the acceleration of cart B is less than the acceleration of cart A.

3. How does mass affect acceleration?

4. What happens to an object if the net force acting on it is zero?

5. How does friction affect motion?

Worksheet 10

Questions 1-3 are based on following description

The diagram represents Earth in its orbit around the Sun. Letters A through D represent Earth on the first day of each season. Letter N represents North Pole. Letter S represents South Pole.

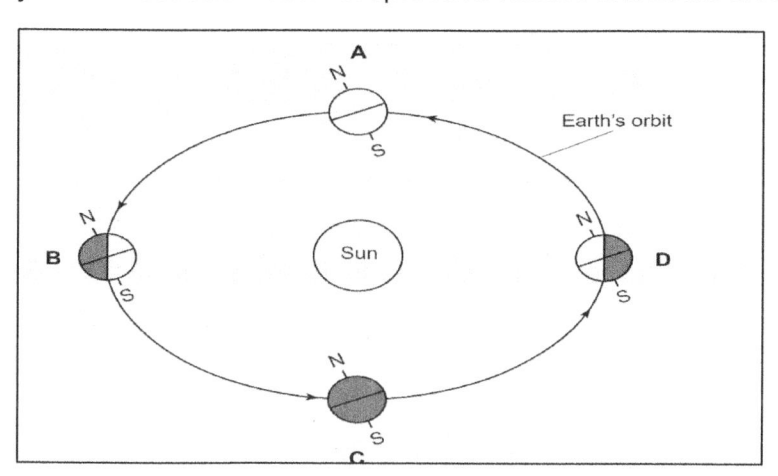

1. Identify the lettered position where an observer in New York State would experience the first day of winter.
   Answer _____

2. Determine the length of time, in months, it takes for Earth to move in its orbit from position A to position B in the diagram.
   Answer _____

3. State one cause of Earth's seasons

4. How do people in the Southern Hemisphere experience the seasons differently from those in the Northern Hemisphere?

5. How does the Earth's distance from the Sun affect seasons?

Worksheet 11

The usage of electricity in the United States has increased dramatically over the past 20 years. Most of this electricity is currently produced by burning fossil fuels.

1. State one reason for this increased usage of electricity.

2. Describe a strategy to reduce the amount of fossil fuels people use in the United States. [1]

3. How can renewable energy sources help reduce our dependence on fossil fuels?

4. What is the difference between renewable and non-renewable sources of electricity?

5. What are the environmental impacts of burning fossil fuels?

Worksheet 12

If 100 offspring were produced from the crossing shown in the Punnett square below, approximately how many would have a wrinkled pod shape?

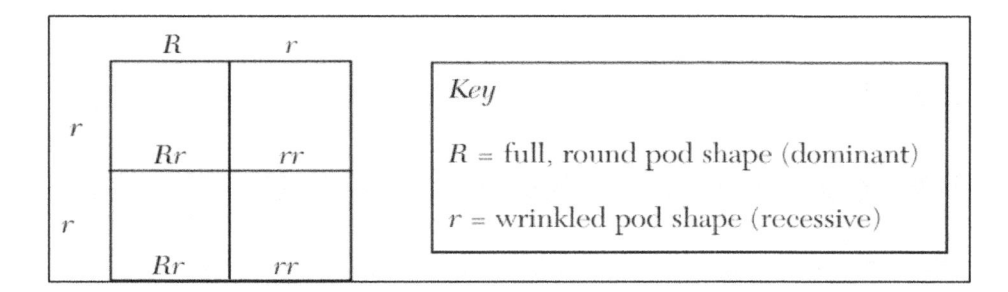

	R	r
r	Rr	rr
r	Rr	rr

Key

R = full, round pod shape (dominant)

r = wrinkled pod shape (recessive)

Base your answers to questions 1 through 4 below, on the diagram below which shows the process of sexual reproduction.

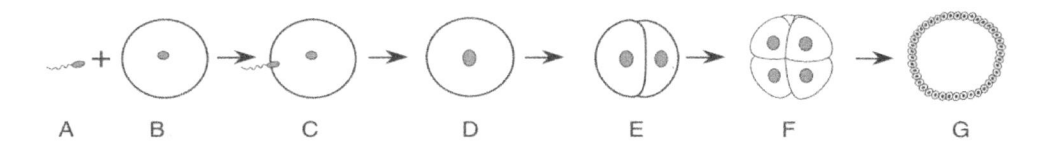

A   B   C   D   E   F   G

1. Identify the sex cell shown at A.

2. Identify the sex cell shown at B

3. Identify the reproductive process that is occurring at C

4. Identify the process that is occurring between E and F.

127

Worksheet 13

1. The two human body systems shown below interact to perform several functions for the whole organism. Describe how gas exchange occurs when the circulatory and respiratory systems work together

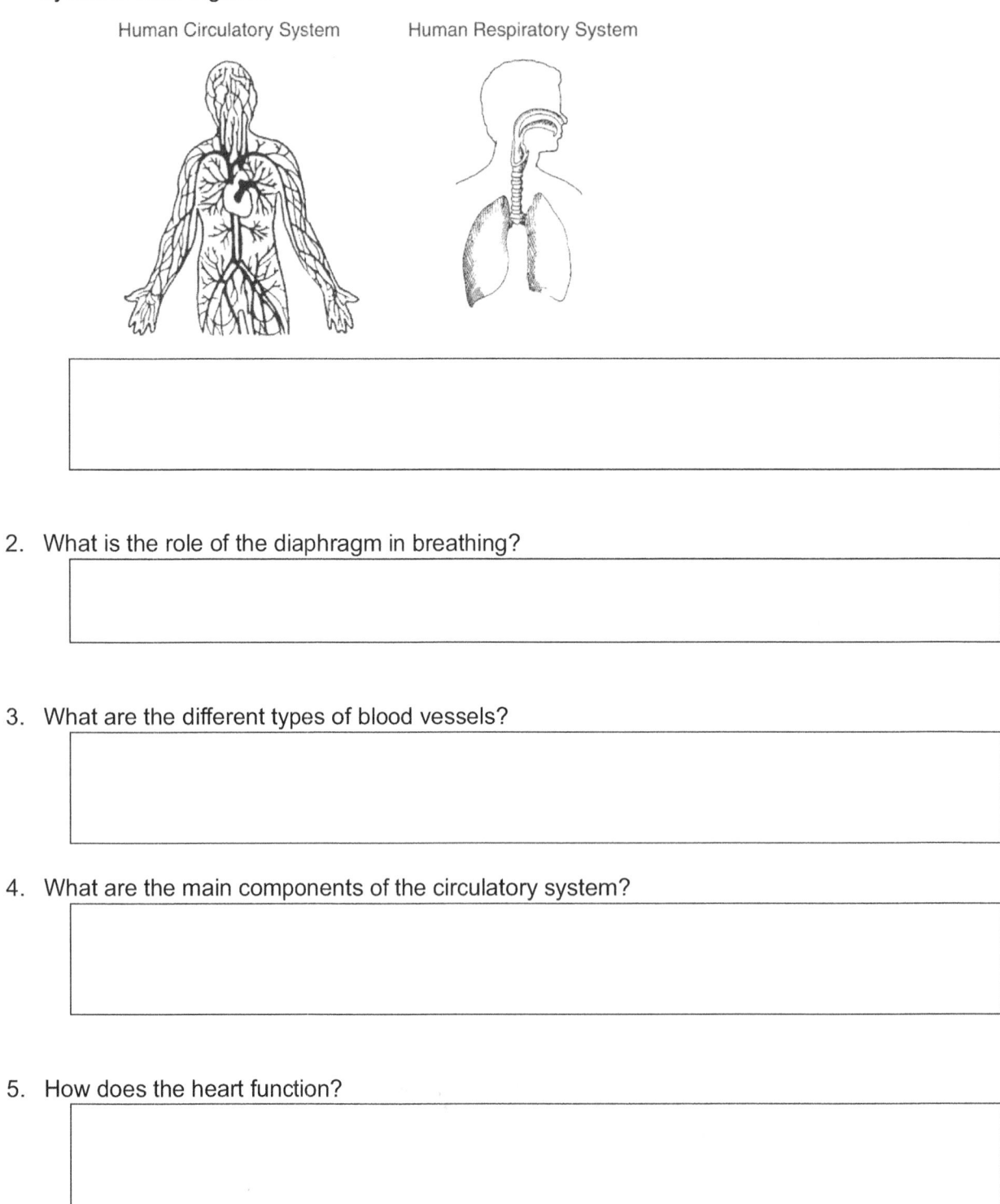

   Human Circulatory System   Human Respiratory System

2. What is the role of the diaphragm in breathing?

3. What are the different types of blood vessels?

4. What are the main components of the circulatory system?

5. How does the heart function?

Worksheet 14

The diagram below shows the rock cycle in Earth's crust. Use this rock cycle diagram to fill in the rock types and method of formation that have been left blank in the chart below.

Rock Cycle in Earth's Crust

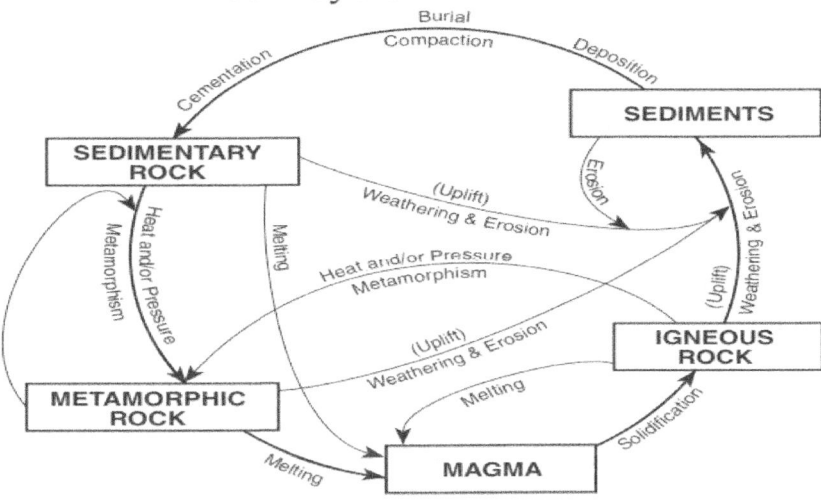

1. **Fill in the missing information in table below**

Rock Type	Method of Formation
	melting and solidification
	deposition, compaction, and cementation
Metamorphic	

2. Why is the rock cycle important?

3. How does human activity impact the rock cycle?

4. How do rocks change from one type to another in the rock cycle?

129

Worksheet 15

The diagram below uses letters A, B, C, and D to represent a water cycle.

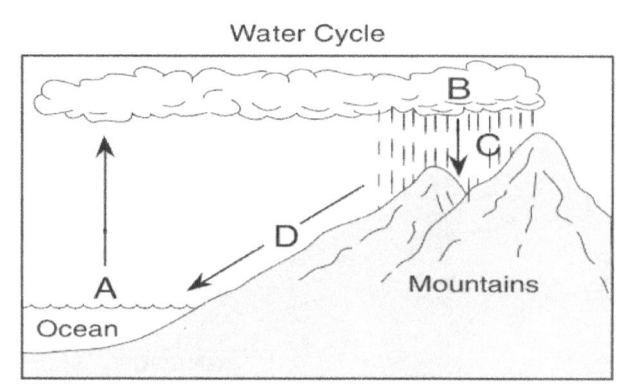

1. In the chart below, identify the process that is occurring at each letter in the diagram. Select the process from the list below.

   Processes: condensation   evaporation   precipitation   runoff

Letter	Process That Is Occurring
A	
B	
C	
D	

2. How does the water cycle affect weather patterns?

3. What is runoff and why is it important?

4. How does infiltration contribute to the water cycle?

Worksheet 16

The diagram shows Earth's revolution around the Sun as viewed from space. Positions A, B, C, and D represent the beginning of each season on Earth.

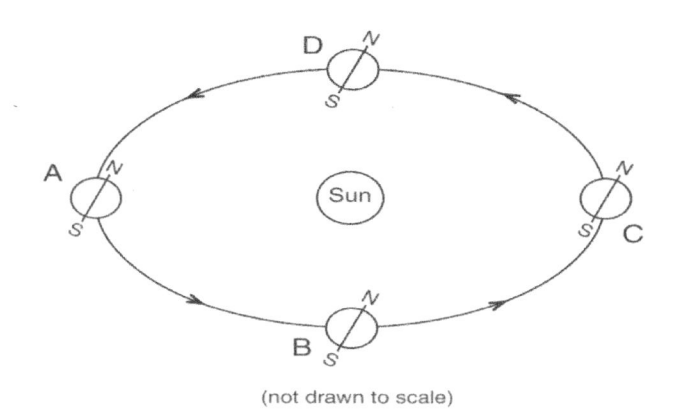

(not drawn to scale)

1. State one reason that Earth has seasons.

2. The axis at points A, B, C, and D are parallel. What is it signifies?

3. If Earth were at position D, how much time would it take to return to position D?

4. Which season begins in the Northern Hemisphere when Earth is at position A?

Worksheet 17

Identify the Criteria and Constraints and possible impacts in following situations

1. You oversee building a footbridge that crosses a small stream. The footbridge must be able to hold the weight of ten people and be 2 meters across and 15 meters in length. The materials for construction must include recycled materials.

Criteria	
Constraints	
Possible impacts	

2. You design a container that keeps a raw egg from cracking when it is dropped 20 feet. You can only use 5 materials in your construction, and you must complete your design and construction in 20 minutes.

Criteria	
Constraints	
Possible impacts	

3. The city has decided to add a dog park to the city lot. It will need fencing, grass, a bench, a bag dispenser, a waste receptacle, and a sign with the rules for dogs and owners. The total cost needs to be under $25,000 dollars

Criteria	
Constraints	
Possible impacts	

Worksheet 18

1. How does the increase in human population affect the number of resources that are consumed?

2. What is a resource that is nonrenewable? Why can't we just make more if this resource?

3. How does the increase in human population affect other organisms on Earth, such fish or birds?

4. How can we promote sustainability in human populations and resource use?

5. How do human activities impact ecosystems and natural resources?

Worksheet 19

1. Sodium sulfate is used to produce many products. Its formula is :

    (Na_2SO_4)

   Which elements are represented in the formula AND how many atoms of each element are represented in the formula?

2. Phosgene is a substance that is often used to make the padding found in car and airplane seats. It is produced when carbon monoxide and chlorine gas react.
   Consider the following reaction:
   1 molecule of carbon monoxide (CO) reacts with 1 molecule of chlorine (Cl2) to produce some amount of phosgene (COCl2).

   To find the amount of phosgene produced, first determine the number of each type of atom in the products.

Chemical element	Number pf atoms in reactants	Number pf atoms in products
C	1	
O	1	
Cl	3	
Explanation		

3. Define reactants and products in a chemical reaction?

4. What is a balanced chemical equation?

Worksheet 20

1. What are the steps of the scientific method?

2. What is a controlled experiment?

3. What is an independent variable, dependent variable, control variable?

4. What are some tips for analyzing data from a scientific experiment?

5. Why is it important to communicate scientific findings?

Answers

Answers to multiple choice questions

Worksheet 1	Worksheet 2	Worksheet 3
1. B	1. A	1. B
2. D	2. C	2. C
3. D	3. D	3. C
4. A and C	4. C	4. A
5. C	5. A and C	5. A
6. D	6. D	6. B
7. B	7. A	7. C
8. C	8. C	8. C
9. C	9. C	9. A
10. D	10. A	10. C
11. C	11. C	11. C
12. A	12. C	12. D
13. A	13. B	13. D
14. C	14. A	14. B
15. C	15. D	15. B

Worksheet 4	Worksheet 5	Worksheet 6
1. B	1. A	1. C
2. B	2. B	2. B
3. D	3. B	3. A
4. C	4. D	4. B
5. C	5. B	5. C
6. B	6. B	6. B
7. A	7. D	7. D
8. C	8. D	8. A
9. A	9. C	9. D
10. D	10. B	10. C
11. A	11. B	11. C
12. C	12. A	12. A
13. B	13. B	13. B
14. A	14. D	14. B
15. B	15. A	15. B

Worksheet 7	Worksheet 8	Worksheet 9
1. D	1. B	1. D
2. D	2. D	2. B
3. B	3. B	3. C
4. A	4. C	4. B
5. D	5. B	5. A
6. A	6. D	6. D
7. C	7. B	7. C
8. C	8. C	8. A
9. B	9. D	9. C
10. B	10. D	10. D
11. A	11. C	11. C
12. B	12. D	12. D
13. D	13. A	13. D
14. B	14. C	14. D
15. C	15. B	15. B

Worksheet 10	Worksheet 11	Worksheet 12
1. C	1. D	1. A
2. D	2. C	2. D
3. B	3. C	3. B and D
4. C	4. B	4. C
5. C	5. D	5. B
6. A	6. C	6. C
7. A	7. A	7. A
8. C	8. A	8. D
9. A	9. D	9. D
10. A	10. D	10. A
11. B	11. A	11. D
12. A	12. B	12. A,B,C,D
13. C	13. A and C	13. A
14. A	14. A	14. D
15. A	15. D	15. A

Worksheet 13	Worksheet 14	Worksheet 15
1. C	1. A	1. C
2. A	2. D	2. B
3. C	3. D	3. A
4. B	4. C	4. C
5. B	5. D	5. A
6. A	6. A	6. B
7. D	7. A and B	7. B
8. B	8. C	8. B
9. C	9. A,B,D	9. A
10. D	10. B	10. D
11. C	11. B	11. C
12. A	12. A	12. C
13. C	13. B	13. C
14. D	14. C	14. A
15. B	15. B	15. B

Performance Tasks and Constructed-Response questions' Answers

The following section provides responses to the constructed-response and performance task questions. While the details written may vary between students, the fundamental explanations should be consistent with the question asked. Folloiwng section gives you the sample answers to each of the question

Worksheet 1
1. The closer the objects, the stronger the gravitational pull. Objects of the same mass, that are closer together will have a stronger pull than objects of the same mass that are further apart.
2. Mass is the amount of matter in an object and is measured in kilograms (kg). It is a scalar quantity and does not change regardless of the object's location. Weight, on the other hand, is the force exerted on an object due to gravity and is measured in newtons (N). Weight depends on the object's mass and the gravitational pull of the location where the object is. Weight can change if the gravitational pull changes, such as when moving from Earth to the Moon.
3. Gravitational pull between larger objects is stronger than gravitational pull between smaller objects (that are the same distance apart).
4. Astronauts orbiting in space feel a sense of weightlessness because there is no external contact force in space pushing or pulling upon their bodies. Gravity is the only force acting upon their body. Gravity being an action-at-a-distance force cannot be felt and therefore would not provide any sensation of weight.
5. Weight W = mg , m= mass and g = gravity For 10 kg object it will be 98 Newtons

Worksheet 2

1. First Law of Motion - Your body will keep moving forward and fly off your skateboard since the curb only stops the board, not yourself. Your body will continue moving until it too is acted upon by a force (like gravity or impact with the sidewalk)
2. We should wear a seatbelt because if the car stops suddenly, your body will keep moving until a force act on it. It is better if this force is a seatbelt than the car itself. This aligns with the first law of motion
3. Inertia: Objects resist change to velocity and direction unless a force acts upon it. This is according to Newton's first law of motion.
4. Forces, when unbalanced, cause objects to accelerate. And the direction of the acceleration is the same as the direction of the extra force.
5. Inertia is resistance to change in motion. The more mass the more inertia an object has. The heavier box would require more force to move it.

Worksheet 3

1. Both involve the passing on of genetic traits through reproduction. Both can include behavioral traits and physical traits.
2. Long ago these two species might have had a common ancestor. Over time, the natural selection process allowed species that were best suited for their environment to survive and pass on their traits. The organisms develop adaptations that functioned well in their environment
3. It is easier for dark grey moths to hid from predators
4. If the pollution control measure increases than there will most likely be less dark grey moths
5. Natural selection can both increase and decrease a population's genetic diversity. It can increase diversity by favoring different traits in different environments, leading to a variety of adaptations. Conversely, it can decrease diversity if only a few traits are highly advantageous, causing those traits to dominate the population while others diminish or disappear.

Worksheet 4

1. The Balloons going to cover more distance with less metal washers
2. The Balloon rocket would travel longer if the circumference is longer and wider. The Circumference is larger that's the more Air in the Balloon
3. Several factors determine the distance a rocket can travel, including:
   - Thrust: The force produced by the rocket engines. Greater thrust can propel the rocket further.
   - Weight: The mass of the rocket. Heavier rockets require more force to travel the same distance as lighter rockets.
   - Fuel Efficiency: How efficiently the rocket uses its fuel. More efficient fuel usage can result in longer travel distances.
   - Aerodynamics: The design of the rocket affects air resistance. More aerodynamic designs reduce drag and increase distance.
   - Gravity: The force of gravity acting on the rocket. In a lower gravity environment, a rocket can travel further.
4. Newton's Third Law of Motion states that for every action, there is an equal and opposite

reaction. For a rocket, the action is the expulsion of gas out of the rocket engine at high speed. The reaction is the thrust force that propels the rocket forward. This means the rocket moves in the opposite direction to the expelled gases, allowing it to accelerate and travel upward.
5. Friction opposes the motion of a moving object, causing it to lose energy and slow down. The greater the frictional force, the shorter the distance the object will travel before coming to a stop. For example, a ball rolling on a rough surface with high friction will stop more quickly than one rolling on a smooth, low-friction surface.

Worksheet 5
1. Plant cell needs cell wall whereas animal cell does not because the plants need rigid structure so that they can grow up and out. All cells have cell membranes, and the membranes are flexible. So animal cells can have various shapes, but plant cells only have the shapes of their cell walls.

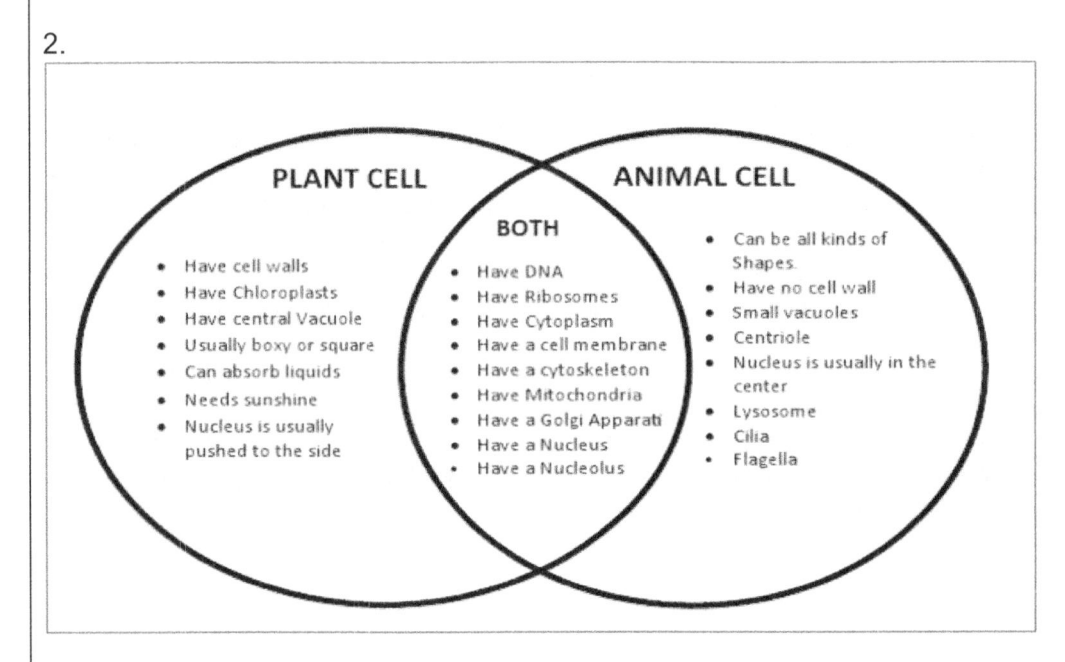

2.

PLANT CELL
- Have cell walls
- Have Chloroplasts
- Have central Vacuole
- Usually boxy or square
- Can absorb liquids
- Needs sunshine
- Nucleus is usually pushed to the side

BOTH
- Have DNA
- Have Ribosomes
- Have Cytoplasm
- Have a cell membrane
- Have a cytoskeleton
- Have Mitochondria
- Have a Golgi Apparati
- Have a Nucleus
- Have a Nucleolus

ANIMAL CELL
- Can be all kinds of Shapes
- Have no cell wall
- Small vacuoles
- Centriole
- Nucleus is usually in the center
- Lysosome
- Cilia
- Flagella

3. The cell membrane, also known as the plasma membrane, is a selectively permeable barrier that surrounds the cell. It regulates the movement of substances in and out of the cell, provides protection, and supports cell communication and signaling. The nucleus is the control center of the cell. It contains the cell's genetic material (DNA) and is responsible for regulating gene expression, cell growth, and reproduction. The nucleus directs all cellular activities by controlling the synthesis of proteins.

4. Chloroplasts are the organelles responsible for photosynthesis in plant cells. They contain the pigment chlorophyll, which captures light energy and converts it into chemical energy through the process of photosynthesis. This process produces glucose and oxygen from carbon dioxide and water.

5. In plant cells, vacuoles are typically large and central, occupying a significant portion of the cell's volume. They store water, nutrients, waste products, and help maintain turgor pressure, which is essential for maintaining the plant's structure and rigidity. In animal cells, vacuoles are smaller and more numerous, and they primarily function in storing and transporting substances within the cell.

Worksheet 6

1. Stratopause 0°C Mesopause 290°C

2. Possible answer: — Water vapor concentration decreases as altitude increases. — an inverse relationship — an indirect relationship — negative correlation

3. Temperature changes with altitude in the atmosphere due to various factors, including the absorption of solar radiation, the composition of gases, and atmospheric pressure. For example, in the troposphere, temperature decreases with altitude because the ground absorbs heat from the Sun and warms the air above it. In the stratosphere, temperature increases with altitude due to the absorption of UV radiation by ozone.

4. The thermosphere extends from about 85 to 600 kilometers (53 to 373 miles) above the Earth's surface. In this layer, temperatures increase significantly with altitude, potentially reaching up to 2,500°C (4,500°F) or higher. Despite the high temperatures, the thermosphere would not feel hot to a human because the air density is extremely low. This layer contains the ionosphere, which is important for radio communication.

5. The ozone layer, located in the lower stratosphere, protects life on Earth by absorbing most of the Sun's harmful ultraviolet (UV) radiation. Without the ozone layer, more UV radiation would reach the Earth's surface, leading to increased risks of skin cancer, cataracts, and other health issues, as well as negative impacts on ecosystems.

Worksheet 7

1. They were the control group. — to compare the plants with the plant food, to the plants without food, to see if there is a difference
2. the plant food.
3. Plants with food were 5 cm taller. — There were two more leaves on the plants that received plant food. — Plants with food were all taller. — The leaves did not turn yellow on the plants with food.

Worksheet 8

1. Repel, Like poles repel. — Two north poles are facing each other
2. The poles of a magnet interact with each other in the following ways:
    - Like Poles Repel: North poles repel other north poles, and south poles repel other south poles.
    - Unlike Poles Attract: North poles attract south poles, and vice versa.

3. You can make a simple electromagnet by following these steps:
    - Take a length of insulated copper wire.
    - Wrap the wire around an iron nail or other iron core several times to create a coil.
    - Connect the ends of the wire to the terminals of a battery.
    - When the electric current flows through the wire, it creates a magnetic field around the nail, turning it into an electromagnet. The magnetism will disappear when the current is turned off.

4. The Earth's magnetic field affects compasses by aligning the magnetic needle with the field. The needle, which is a small magnet, aligns itself so that one end points toward the magnetic north pole and the other end points toward the magnetic south pole. This allows a compass to indicate direction relative to the Earth's magnetic field.
5. Magnetic induction, or electromagnetic induction, is the process by which a changing magnetic field within a coil of wire induces an electric current in the wire. This principle is used in generators to produce electricity and in transformers to transfer electrical energy between circuits.

Worksheet 9

1. 2.0 m per second squared
2. The total mass of cart B is greater. — A 2-kg mass was added to the cart. — Cart B is heavier.
3. Mass affects acceleration according to Newton's Second Law of Motion, which states that the force applied to an object is equal to the mass of the object times its acceleration (F=ma). For a given force, an object with greater mass will have a smaller acceleration, while an object with less mass will have a greater acceleration.
4. If the net force acting on an object is zero, the object will either remain at rest if it was initially stationary or continue to move at a constant velocity if it was already in motion. This is described by Newton's First Law of Motion, also known as the law of inertia.
5. Friction affects motion by resisting the movement of objects. It can slow down or stop the motion of objects in contact with each other. For example, friction between a car's tires and the road surface allows the car to brake and come to a stop. Without friction, objects would continue to move indefinitely once set in motion.

Worksheet 10

1. B
2. 3 months
3. Earth revolves around/orbits the Sun. — tilt of Earth's axis — parallelism of Earth's tilted axis — changing angle of the Sun's incoming rays
4. People in the Southern Hemisphere experience the seasons opposite to those in the Northern Hemisphere. For example, when it is summer in the Northern Hemisphere (around June), it is winter in the Southern Hemisphere. This is because the tilt of the Earth's axis causes one hemisphere to receive more direct sunlight while the other receives less, resulting in opposite seasonal patterns.
5. The Earth's distance from the Sun does have a small effect on the seasons, but it is not

the primary cause. The Earth's orbit is slightly elliptical, so there are times when it is slightly closer (perihelion) and times when it is slightly farther (aphelion) from the Sun. However, the tilt of the Earth's axis has a much larger influence on the seasons.

Worksheet 11

1. A correct reason for increased usage is provided, along with specific examples, such as increased use of technology and increased population.
2. Correct conservation measures include: ☐ lowering thermostats ☐ replacing windows ☐ using a wood stove ☐ educational campaign about lowering electricity use ☐ use alternative energy sources ☐ use public transportation/car pool ☐ turning off lights ☐ using energy efficient appliances
3. Renewable energy sources like solar, wind, and hydroelectric power can help reduce our dependence on fossil fuels by providing a clean and sustainable alternative. These sources produce little to no greenhouse gases or air pollution, helping to mitigate climate change and improve air quality. Transitioning to renewable energy also promotes energy independence and creates new job opportunities in the clean energy sector.
4. Non-Renewable Sources: Non-renewable sources like fossil fuels and nuclear energy are finite and will eventually run out. They also have negative environmental impacts. Renewable Sources: Renewable sources like solar, wind, hydro, and geothermal energy are naturally replenished and won't run out. They also have minimal or no negative environmental impacts.
5. Burning fossil fuels releases carbon dioxide and other greenhouse gases into the atmosphere, contributing to global warming and climate change. It also causes air pollution, including smog, acid rain, and health problems.

Worksheet 12

1. Correct answer: sperm, male sex cell Incorrect answer: semen
2. Correct answer   egg, ovum, female sex cell
3. Correct answer fertilization Incorrect answer: The sperm enters the egg.
4. Correct answer   — cell division — mitosis — binary fission/fission — cells splitting — reproduction of the cells — cell multiplication Incorrect answers: duplication; the egg is breaking up; the egg is splitting; egg dividing; egg developing; egg multiplying

Worksheet 13

1. Correct answers include: — The respiratory system brings oxygen into the body and the circulatory system carries oxygen to the cells. — The circulatory system carries carbon dioxide away from the cells and the respiratory system moves carbon dioxide out of the body. — The oxygen is brought from the lungs to the other parts of the body by the blood and it picks up CO2 and you breathe it out. — The air is pushed through the respiratory system and carried through the blood in the circulatory system.
2. The diaphragm is a dome-shaped muscle below the lungs. When it contracts, it moves downward, increasing the space in the chest cavity and causing inhalation (breathing in). When it relaxes, it moves upward, decreasing the space in the chest cavity and causing exhalation (breathing out).
3. There are three main types of blood vessels:
    - Arteries: Carry oxygen-rich blood away from the heart to the body.
    - Veins: Carry oxygen-poor blood back to the heart.

- Capillaries: Small blood vessels that connect arteries and veins and allow for the exchange of gases, nutrients, and waste products with body tissues.
4. The main components of the circulatory system include:
    - Heart: A muscular organ that pumps blood throughout the body.
    - Blood Vessels: Tubes that carry blood throughout the body. They include arteries, veins, and capillaries.
    - Blood: A fluid that carries nutrients, oxygen, carbon dioxide, hormones, and waste products throughout the body.
5. The heart functions as a pump to circulate blood throughout the body. It consists of four chambers: two atria (upper chambers) and two ventricles (lower chambers). Blood flows from the body into the right atrium, then into the right ventricle, where it is pumped to the lungs to pick up oxygen. Oxygen-rich blood returns to the left atrium, then to the left ventricle, which pumps it out to the rest of the body.

Worksheet 14

1.

Rock Type	Method of Formation
Igneous	melting and solidification
Sedimentary	deposition, compaction, and cementation
Metamorphic	— **heat and/or pressure** — **metamorphism**

Note: Do *not* accept "magma" for igneous.
Do *not* accept "sediments" for sedimentary.
Do *not* accept "melting" for heat and/or pressure.

2. The rock cycle is important because it illustrates how Earth's materials are recycled and transformed over time. It plays a crucial role in shaping the Earth's crust, creating new landforms, and providing resources essential for human activities.
3. Human activity can impact the rock cycle through activities such as mining and quarrying, which extract large amounts of rocks and minerals. Deforestation and construction also affect weathering and erosion rates, altering natural rock cycle processes.
4. Rocks change from one type to another in the rock cycle through a combination of geological processes. For example:
    - Igneous rocks can be weathered and eroded into sediments, which then undergo compaction and cementation to form sedimentary rocks.
    - Any type of rock can be subjected to heat and pressure, causing it to undergo metamorphism and become metamorphic rock.
    - Any type of rock can melt into magma, which can then cool and solidify to form igneous rock.

Worksheet 15

Letter	Process That is Occurring
A	evaporation
B	condensation
C	precipitation
D	runoff

1.
2. The water cycle affects weather patterns by distributing heat and moisture around the Earth. Evaporation and transpiration release water vapor into the atmosphere, which can form clouds and precipitation. This influences temperature, humidity, and precipitation patterns globally.
3. Runoff is the flow of water over the Earth's surface and into bodies of water such as rivers, lakes, and oceans. It is important because it replenishes freshwater sources and helps regulate the Earth's water cycle.
4. Infiltration is the process by which water seeps into the ground and becomes groundwater. It contributes to the water cycle by replenishing underground water sources and eventually re-entering the surface water through springs and streams.

Worksheet 16

1. tilt of axis — revolution —
2. Rotation
3. Any of following answer is correct — one year — 365 days — 365.25 days — 365 ¼ days — 4 seasons — 12 months
4. Correct answer summer. Note: Credit not given for -- June, July, or August.

Worksheet 17

1.
   - Criteria: Hold the weight of ten people, 2 meters across, 15 meters in length.
   - Constraints   The materials must include recycled materials
   - Possible Impacts: Perhaps it will keep people from wading through the stream. It is positive that recycled materials will be used

2.
   - Criteria: Dropped 20 feet and doesn't crack.
   - Constraints   Only use 5 materials must complete in 20 minutes
   - Possible Impacts: No negative impacts

3.
   - Criteria: Fencing, grass, bench, bag dispenser, waste receptacle, and sign.
   - Constraints   Under $25,000
   - Possible Impacts: Positive for health of humans and dogs

Worksheet 18

1. The more humans there are, the more demand for resources of energy, food, water, and space for humans to use. More humans use more resources
2. One resources that is nonrenewable is natural gas. Natural gas is a non-renewable fossil fuel formed from the remains of tiny sea plants and animals that died 300-400 million years ago. It would take millions of years to produce new natural gas from today's see organisms.
3. Other organisms like birds and fish must compete with humans for habitat and food. Also, human produced pollution affects birds and fish, making them sick. In addition, overharvesting of birds and fish for food or other products can reduce populations of birds and fish
4. We can promote sustainability through practices such as:
    - Conserving energy and water.
    - Reducing, reusing, and recycling materials.
    - Protecting and restoring ecosystems and biodiversity.
    - Using renewable energy sources.
    - Promoting sustainable agriculture and fishing practices.
    - Educating and raising awareness about environmental issues and sustainable living.
5. Human activities impact ecosystems and natural resources through activities such as deforestation, pollution, overfishing, and urbanization. These activities can lead to habitat destruction, loss of biodiversity, and depletion of natural resources.

Worksheet 19

1. There are a total of 7 atoms representing three elements in the formula AND • The elements are sodium (2 atoms), sulfur (1 atom), and oxygen (4 atoms)
2. The number and type of atoms in the products are the *same* as the number and type of atoms that were in the reactants. This means that the number of each type of atom is the *same* in the products and in the reactants. here are 1 carbon atom, 1 oxygen atom, and 2 chlorine atoms in the reactants. So, there are also **1 carbon atom, 1 oxygen atom, and 2 chlorine atoms** in the products.
3. **Reactants** are the starting substances that undergo a chemical change during a reaction. They are found on the left side of a chemical equation.
   Products are the substances that are formed as a result of a chemical reaction. They are found on the right side of a chemical equation.
4. A chemical equation is balanced when the number of atoms of each element is the same on both sides of the equation. This reflects the law of conservation of mass, which states that matter cannot be created or destroyed in a chemical reaction.
   To balance a chemical equation:
   - Write the unbalanced equation.
   - Count the number of atoms of each element on both sides.
   - Add coefficients (whole numbers) in front of the reactants and products to balance the number of atoms for each element.
   - Check that all atoms balance and adjust coefficients if necessary.

Worksheet 20

1. The steps of the scientific method are:

   - Observation: Noticing and describing an event or phenomenon.
   - Question: Asking a question about the observation.
   - Hypothesis: Proposing a tentative explanation based on the observation.
   - Prediction: Making a prediction based on the hypothesis.
   - Experiment: Testing the hypothesis through controlled experiments.
   - Analysis: Analyzing and interpreting data collected from the experiment.
   - Conclusion: Drawing a conclusion based on the data and determining if the hypothesis was supported or not.

2. A **controlled experiment** is an experiment where all variables except the one being tested are kept constant. This allows scientists to isolate the effect of the variable being tested.

3. An **independent** variable is the variable that is changed or manipulated in an experiment to observe its effect on the dependent variable. A **dependent** variable is the variable that is measured or observed in an experiment. It is affected by changes in the independent variable.
   A **control** variable is a variable that is kept constant and unchanged throughout the experiment to ensure that only the independent variable affects the dependent variable.

4. Some tips for analyzing data from a scientific experiment include:

   - Organize data: Use tables, graphs, or charts to organize data for easy comparison.
   - Identify patterns: Look for trends or patterns in the data.
   - Calculate averages: Calculate averages or means to summarize data.
   - Draw conclusions: Compare results to predictions and draw conclusions based on the data.
   - Consider limitations: Consider any limitations or sources of error in the experiment.

5. It is important to communicate scientific findings to share knowledge, validate results, and enable others to build on existing research. Communication allows scientists to collaborate, replicate experiments, and advance scientific understanding.

Author's message:

Dear Young Scientists,

Welcome to "Mastering CAST - California Science Test for Grade 8"! This book has been created with you in mind, to help you succeed in your science journey and excel on your state science test. But more than that, we hope this book will inspire a love for science and a sense of wonder about the world around you.

Science is a subject full of discoveries and exciting opportunities to learn about the world and how it works. Through the pages of this book, you'll explore concepts from Earth and space sciences, life sciences, and physical sciences. You'll practice solving problems, think critically, and test your knowledge with a variety of engaging questions.

Remember, science is not just about finding the right answers—it's about asking questions, observing, experimenting, and making connections. Whether you're learning about the water cycle, ecosystems, or the laws of motion, you are developing skills that will help you throughout your life.

As you work through the book, don't be afraid to make mistakes. Making mistakes is an important part of the learning process. Each challenge you overcome and each lesson you learn will make you a stronger and more confident scientist.

Most importantly, have fun! Enjoy the process of discovering new things and challenging yourself. Your curiosity is your greatest tool in science.

Best of luck on your journey to mastering science! We believe in your ability to succeed and are excited to see what amazing things you'll accomplish.

Happy exploring!

Karry

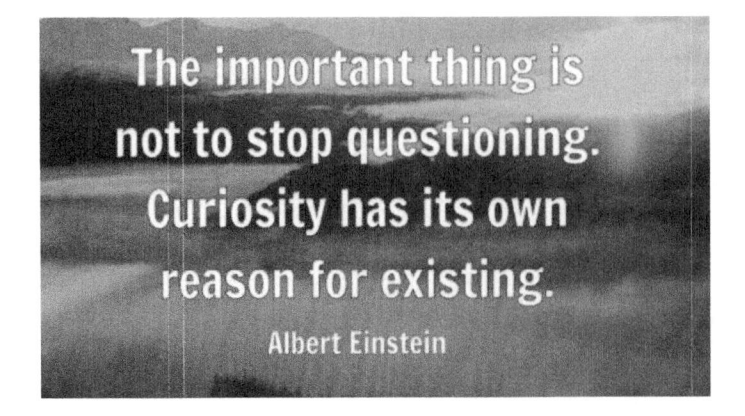

> The important thing is not to stop questioning. Curiosity has its own reason for existing.
> — Albert Einstein